KEEPING THE U.S. COMPUTER INDUSTRY COMPETITIVE: SYSTEMS INTEGRATION

A COLLOQUIUM REPORT BY

THE COMPUTER SCIENCE AND TELECOMMUNICATIONS BOARD

COMMISSION ON PHYSICAL SCIENCES, MATHEMATICS, AND APPLICATIONS

NATIONAL RESEARCH COUNCIL

NATIONAL ACADEMY PRESS
WASHINGTON, D.C. 1992

Support for this project was provided by the following organizations and agencies: Air Force Office of Scientific Research (Grant No. N00014-87-J-1110), Apple Computer, Inc., Control Data Corporation, Cray Research, Inc., the Defense Advanced Research Projects Agency (Grant No. N00014-87-J-1110), Digital Equipment Corporation, Hewlett Packard, IBM Corpo-ration, the National Aeronautics and Space Administration (Grant No. CDA-860535), the Na-tional Science Foundation (Grant No. CDA-860535), the Office of Naval Research (Grant No. N00014-87-J-1110), and Pacific Bell.

Library of Congress Catalog Card Number 91-62172
International Standard Book Number 0-309-04544-4

Available from:

National Academy Press
2101 Constitution Avenue, NW
Washington, DC 20418

S404

Printed in the United States of America

Preface

This report on systems integration is the second in a series of Computer Science and Telecommunications Board (CSTB) reports focusing on the competitive status of the U.S. computer industry. In CSTB's initial report, *Keeping the U.S. Computer Industry Competitive: Defining the Agenda* (National Academy Press, Washington, D.C., 1990), leaders of the computing field surveyed each of the major sectors of the computer industry. To no one's surprise, the hardware sector was considered to be under serious competitive pressure, with the semiconductor memory market all but ceded to Japanese companies. The U.S. competitive position in the software market was deemed to be strong but precarious, given the weakness in basic hardware components. However, systems integration was identified as a large and rapidly growing market in which the United States was a clear leader; unfortunately, few could agree on just what systems integration was!

The present report is based on a colloquium held in January 1991 in which participants from industry, academia, and government discussed what systems integration is, its importance and prospects for growth, and why the United States is perceived to have a strong competitive advantage. A distillation of the colloquium discussions, this report is designed, in particular, to inform policymakers, but it should also be of value to anyone with an interest in computing and telecommunications.

The colloquium was organized by a steering committee chaired by Laszlo Belady, then vice president for Software Technology and Advanced Computing Technology Programs at the Microelectronics and Computer Technology Corporation (he is now chairman and director of Mitsubishi Electric Research Laboratories Inc.). Other members of the steering committee were Samuel Fuller, vice president of research at Digital Equipment Corporation; Robert Lucky, executive director of research, Communications Sciences Division, AT&T Bell Laboratories; and Irving Wladawsky-Berger, assistant general manager of development and quality for IBM's Enterprise Systems. Among CSTB staff, Damian Saccocio and Catherine Sparks had principal responsibility for the colloquium; they were aided by CSTB meeting consultant Pamela Rodgers and free-lance science writer Mark Bello.

Joseph F. Traub, *Chairman*
Computer Science and
Telecommunications Board

Contents

Executive Summary

Systems integration offers an enormous opportunity for U.S. firms to capitalize on their strengths in such areas as complex software, networking, and management. Although no single definition of systems integration is complete, it can be broadly considered as the "wiring" together, via hardware and frequently very complex software, of the often already existing islands of computer applications into a coordinated enterprise-wide distributed network system. As this formulation suggests, the fundamental challenges raised by systems integration are those associated with building large systems from heterogeneous components. There is a growing demand for such systems, and a growing need to overcome the vexing challenges inherent in their design and development. At a January 1991 colloquium organized by the Computer Science and Telecommunications Board of the National Research Council, industry leaders, university researchers, and government policymakers discussed how systems integration is taking shape today and why it is expected to define the characteristics of computerization for decades to come.

Systems integration can be viewed as a culmination of computing and communications research done to date. To fulfill the promise of systems integration, a wide range of component technologies—including databases, operating systems, architectures, networks, security mechanisms, human interfaces, artificial intelligence, and communications—must work together. Expertise about the many domains in which systems integration is applied (finance, retail, transportation, and so on) must also be invoked. Thus an interdisciplinary approach is essential to successful systems integration, as are complementary and coordinated research and development efforts in industry, academia, and government. Toward both ends, colloquium participants urged that universities pay more attention to systems integration in devising educational and research programs in computing and communications.

The technological challenges encompassed in systems integration are formidable, but for the moment they play to U.S. strengths. For example, much of systems integration depends on the development of sophisticated and often highly specialized software—a difficult process but one in which the United States is preeminent. Other key abilities essential to successful systems integration, also abilities in which the United States excels, include creative problem solving and management of complex, often one-of-a-kind processes.

One area in which the U.S. record is mixed is that of standards setting. The continued development of systems integration as an industry depends fundamentally on the compatibility of component technologies. Therefore standards of interoperability are indispensable. Colloquium participants were uniform in urging that more attention be paid to the standards-making process—by government as well as by industry.

Systems integration involves more than technology: its highest-order task is integrating people—helping them assimilate information, create, collaborate, and, in sum, work more productively. While networks of machines and devices are the ostensible manifestations of the trend toward distributed computing and communications, the most significant connections, according to colloquium participants, are those between people and organizational units using linked devices. For this reason, systems integration technology, and in particular the successful building and operation of networked computer applications, is considered key to the emergence of an information infrastructure for the nation (and the world).

Colloquium participants expressed both hope and concern for the anticipated information infrastructure. The quality of that infrastructure, as well as its timely development, hinges on leadership and vision; this was a principal area of agreement among participants. It also hinges on constructive collaboration among industry, government, and academia. The federal High Performance Computing and Communications (HPCC) program was recognized by participants as a key step toward developing this infrastructure and as a valuable mechanism for fostering interactions among government, industry, and academia. Other federal projects, including systems modernization at government agencies, could also serve to demonstrate applications of systems integration and options for cross-sectoral collaboration.

The United States faces a peculiar challenge in the evolution of its computing, telecommunications, and broadcast media infrastructure. The quality and availability of U.S. telephone service, entertainment, and business computing are unparalleled. But because it was the first country to embrace many of these new technologies, the United States must now build on a rapidly aging (by the standards of information technology development today) foundation. The huge installed technology base is both an engine for current activities and a constraint on the development and implementation of new technologies; obtaining the benefit of the new with minimal disruption to ongoing activities that depend on the old is no small challenge.

One important factor in the evolution of information infrastructure is the body of U.S. telecommunications regulations. Colloquium participants observed that those regulations may not have kept pace with changing technologies and industry boundaries. In particular, the proliferation of digital technology into communications results in an effective convergence of computing, communications, and entertainment (programming) industries that raises new questions about fairness, competitive conduct, and other concerns long addressed through telecommunications regulations.

As the predominantly digital technologies essential for systems integration continue to mature, the focus of activity in systems integration may shift from creating a solution to a problem to engineering that solution. This change in focus may allow foreign competitors who excel in engineering and implementation but not necessarily in devising innovative solutions an opportunity to enter the systems integration market. U.S. systems integration firms thus should not be content with being first to market, nor sanguine in their belief in the "American" nature of the industry. U.S. high-technology industries are rife with instances in which American leadership was supplanted by superior production from abroad. Moreover, colloquium participants observed that foreign countries, most notably Japan and countries in Western Europe, have been developing their information infrastructures with greater levels of determination and comprehensiveness than those exhibited thus far in the United States.

To date, systems integration has been a success story. It is time that government, industry, and academia collectively acknowledge the value of systems integration and act to assure the ongoing vitality and competitiveness of U.S. technical and commercial activities in systems integration.

1

Overview

Now into its fifth decade, the so-called computer age has wrought an expectation of rapid technological progress. In fact, the sustained pace of rapid advance in hardware has become formulaic. The storage capacity of dynamic random access memory chips quadruples about every four years, processing speeds increase at double-digit annual rates, and the cost of computing declines between 20 and 30 percent each year. Add to these computing trends a growing array of digital communication devices and related technologies, and the raw capabilities of modern information technology can astound. Indeed, the technology—from automatic teller machines to laser scanning at the checkout stand to desktop publishing and to global distributed computing networks—has transformed spheres of business and many other areas of human endeavor. To many, today's applications are early manifestations of a seemingly endless stream of possibilities flowing from the font of information technology.

Still, society's appreciation, mastery, and application of information technology have grown more slowly and more fitfully than have the power and potential of hardware. The learning curve associated with the technology has proved to be steep. But organizations that have managed to move high up on the curve are reaping substantial benefits. These organizations have advanced beyond using computers to automate existing processes and have proceeded to enterprise-wide systems integration. Capitalizing on the convergence of computer and communications technology, they use hardware and very complex software to connect islands of computer applications into coordinated distributed network systems that often are global in reach. The integration entails far more than systems engineering—the physical linkage of disparate and once-incompatible technologies. It involves melding application domains, such as manufacturing, finance, retail, or transportation, with a supporting infrastructure of information technology components, including databases, operating systems, architectures, networks, communications devices, and security measures. The result is a transformation of the business environment and of business processes, a strategic change aimed at rapid capture and assimilation of information for planning and decision making.

Today, executives and researchers speak of "learning organizations" and of the need for businesses to "reinvent" themselves as competitive conditions change. Both concepts reflect the critically important enabling role played by information technology.

Systems integration represents, in effect, the fruitful culmination of computing and communications research and experience, and it is digital technology's point of departure into the information age. "If there is any trend that has been consistent over the last four decades of computation, it is integration," explained Laszlo Belady, former vice president for software technology and advanced computing technology at the Microelectronics and Computer Technology Corp. (he is now chairman and director of Mitsubishi Electric Research Laboratories Inc.). "Forty years ago," he continued, "everything was isolated in terms of computer use—isolated in space and time. Now we see that both dimensions are integrated. There is continuity in electronic information, in time, and more and more applications have become interconnected. This leads to distributed computing networks."

Some U.S. businesses and government organizations are investing heavily in their information futures. Corporate spending for private networks now accounts for more than half of all investment in U.S. communications networks.[1] This has spawned an amalgam of uncoordinated networking initiatives, but many organizations remain untethered to the electronic connections that have sprouted over the last decade. Some small and midsize companies have formed information partnerships and pooled their resources to overcome the large financial and technical obstacles to exploiting the advantages of integrating and linking their information technology.[2] Most have not.

Many observers believe that the United States must build a national information infrastructure and that this information-age equivalent of the national highway system will not materialize from the ad hoc networks that have emerged in recent years. Advocates, including members of the Computer Science and Telecommunications Board, believe that the potential benefits wrought by new digital technology—as well as those to come, when information in all its diverse textual, graphic, and audio forms can be transmitted electronically—will multiply if the economy and all of society are integrated into a cohesive nationwide network with links to the rest of the world.[3]

In January 1991, the Computer Science and Telecommunications Board (CSTB) of the National Research Council sponsored a colloquium to contemplate the future of systems integration on scales small and large. Participants included representatives of manufacturers of information technology, systems integration firms, and businesses that are heavy users of information technology; government agencies; and universities.

In particular, participants evaluated the implications of the trend toward distributed computing networks for the U.S. computer and telecommunications industries. More generally, they assessed the significance of this trend for the U.S. economy and debated the roles of government, industry, and universities in developing a nationwide information infrastructure, a computing and communications network with universal access.

This report summarizes the proceedings of the day-long colloquium. Supplementary materials, referenced in the text, were used to augment or amplify the points made by participants. The remainder of this chapter provides a historical overview of the systems integration industry and of the trends underlying the growth of distributed computing networks. Chapter 2 describes applications of integrated information systems in business, as well as the challenges that information networking poses. Enabling technology, especially software and communications technology, is the focus of Chapter 3. In Chapter 4, views of the future and the evolution of today's information networks into systems of systems are discussed. The final chapter summarizes the main issues and themes that emerged during the colloquium.

EVOLUTION OF A U.S. BUSINESS CONCEPT

Like the computer and the telephone, systems integration is a product of U.S. innovation. Its roots can be traced to the 1960s, when federal agencies first contracted with firms to design large-scale systems for data processing, communications, and aerospace and defense applications. Opportunities in the commercial sector grew in step with advances in computing technology and with the proliferation of proprietary hardware and software products. Some business customers persisted with a single vendor, assuming, sometimes incorrectly, compatibility across different families and generations of products. Requiring features or applications not offered by the supplier of their original equipment or responding to better price offerings, other customers picked and chose among rival vendors and became the owners of collections of incompatible hardware and software items. In addition, many organizations developed their own customized software applications. With each passing year, it became increasingly difficult to incorporate new technology into the existing base of hardware, software, and databases.

User demand for connectivity of hardware fueled the growth of systems engineering businesses, as did the emergence of affordable desktop machines, which led to what has been described as the democratization of computing. Subsequent demand for interoperability of software applications created new business opportunities. From these beginnings and with the aid of the computer industry's gradual and still-continuing migration to open architectures and networking standards, systems engineering evolved into systems integration, a more robust and more comprehensive undertaking that goes beyond making incompatible machines "talk" to each other. Today, systems integration is recognized as a *problem-solving activity* that entails harnessing and coordinating the power and capabilities of information technology in ways tailored to meet a customer's well-defined set of needs. The result is a complex one-of-a-kind system that, for a business, is intended to increase productivity, flexibility, responsiveness, and, ultimately, competitive advantage. Value is derived from the ability to achieve system-wide synergy among the technological elements and among the people linked by the network.

Typically, the end products are "large complex applications" built with a "broad range of knowledge," explained Ivan Selin, then under secretary for management in the U.S. Department of State (he is now chairman of the Nuclear Regulatory Commission). "Although hardware and software may be the bulk of what is delivered, there is a lot of consulting, a lot of modification, interfacing, coding, installing—making this operation work in a large application," he said. Such work requires an interdisciplinary approach that includes not only hardware and software experts but also experts in the application domain for which the system is being developed (e.g., in a steel foundry it is vital to include individuals who understand steel manufacturing). According to Selin, founder of the systems integration firm American Management Systems, "know-how" is the primary source of value added.

STATUS OF THE U.S. INDUSTRY

Unlike some other segments of the U.S. computer sector, the systems integration industry is thriving and is positioned well ahead of still-embryonic foreign competition. In 1990, the systems integration industry had estimated revenues of $14.9 billion; revenues in 1991 were projected to grow 13 percent to $16.8 billion.[4] Enlarging foreign markets, especially Europe, are expected to drive rapid revenue increases during the next five years.[5]

About 1,600 firms earn all or the bulk of their revenues from systems integration. The largest of these include Electronic Data Systems, a subsidiary of General Motors with annual revenues of almost $6 billion, and Andersen Consulting, a division of the accounting firm Arthur Andersen & Co. Among the newest competitors in the commercial market are defense firms that have developed their systems integration expertise in designing and developing complex computer-controlled weapons systems or parts of the U.S. military's sophisticated command, control, communication, and intelligence networks.

In an industry traditionally structured to sell hardware components and supporting software products, systems integration is having profound effects on business strategy. Companies are maneuvering to meet the demands and needs of droves of customers who are linking their information technology into networks. In 1990 alone, U.S. businesses connected nearly 4 million personal computers to local networks, bringing the total number of networked PCs to more than 11 million.[6]

Many companies already providing computing and communication products and services have pegged systems integration and networked computing as key growth areas. Examples include the International Business Machines Corp., American Telephone & Telegraph Co., Digital Equipment Corp., Xerox Corp., Hewlett-Packard Co., Unisys, Motorola Inc., Compaq, and the NCR Corp. (which recently merged with AT&T). Major independent software publishers—among them Microsoft, the Lotus Development Corp., Computer Associates International, and the Oracle Corp.—have followed suit and have made networking applications a priority. Also vying in the market are retailer Sears, aircraft manufacturers McDonnell Douglas and Boeing, and accounting firms Arthur Andersen & Co., Price Waterhouse, Ernst and Young, and KPMG Peat Marwick. These and other firms with considerable experience in building and managing complex systems of information technology to support their main lines of business have created separate divisions to market their systems integration expertise.

Sometimes called flexible partnerships, alliances among firms are common. On one project, companies with complementary expertise may combine their resources and skills, but on another former partners may vie as competitors. Moreover, large businesses with in-house personnel assigned to building and managing information systems may call on outside firms for needed expertise in particular areas.

The strategic importance of systems integration and prospects for continuing high rates of systems integration are influencing both the behavior and structure of the computer and communications industries. In increasing numbers, hardware and software manufacturers are moving away from building proprietary equipment and applications and committing themselves to "open systems"—making software and hardware that conform with industry-accepted standards and, therefore, can work with the offerings of other vendors.

Recent acquisitions provide further evidence of the profound influence of systems integration and information networking. The most notable, perhaps, is AT&T's purchase of the NCR Corp., the nation's fifth-largest computer manufacturer. A prime motivation behind AT&T's prolonged but eventually successful takeover, AT&T Chairman Robert E. Allen was quoted as saying, was to create a company capable of providing "global networks as easy to use and as accessible as the telephone network is today."[7] Also acting to strengthen its competitive position in the market for networking applications and services, the Lotus Development Corp., one of the country's largest independent software publishers, purchased cc:Mail, a company with expertise in electronic mail applications. Previously, Lotus and Novell Inc., the largest maker of software for managing networks of personal computers, had explored the possibility of a merger, another indication of how companies are maneuvering to compete in the growing market for intra- and inter-networking products and services.

Global Prospects

Systems integration remains largely an American phenomenon, but one that has captured the attention of foreign businesses—as customers and as competitors. Although beginning from a small base, foreign sales represent the fastest-growing market segment for some established U.S. systems integration businesses. Opportunities in foreign markets are likely to stimulate local competition, as well as draw new international competitors. Several colloquium participants said that they anticipated greater interest from Japanese electronics and telecommunication conglomerates, such as Toshiba, Fujitsu, NEC, Nippon Telephone and Telegraph, and Hitachi, each with annual revenues in excess of $10 billion. In Europe, cooperative government-sponsored research and development projects focusing on future computing and telecommunications technologies raise the specter of greater local competition in that lucrative market.

Despite the expectation that foreign firms will make a determined push in global markets for systems integration services, Belady and other colloquium participants suggested that at this stage in the evolution of information technology, the emerging opportunities are there for U.S. firms to lose. Systems integration, said Selin, is a "particularly strong example of [a] uniquely American ability to solve one-of-a-kind problems or solve very complex, very difficult problems in ways that are very hard to imagine. . . . [W]e're very effective when it comes to providing technological solutions to difficult problems."

For now, Selin added, the U.S. systems integration industry benefits from demonstrable successes that have made it the "recognized world leader." Because of U.S. accomplishments in designing, developing, and implementing large computer and communications systems, "being an American is a big advantage, not a disadvantage [as it is in] a number of other parts of our industry," he said.

Charles S. Feld, vice president for management information systems at Frito-Lay Inc., also noted a significant gap between the systems integration capabilities of U.S. companies and those of foreign firms. Having built an advanced information network that links all elements of its domestic operations, Frito-Lay intends to build a counterpart for its expanding international business, which has units in 22 countries. The task has proved to be very challenging. In his visits to foreign operations acquired by Frito-Lay, Feld has found that, "even though the hardware is exactly the same as what we would be using here, it is like being back in the 1960s in terms of the way people do projects and the way they think about things. I think we really do have a national asset here that is tremendous."

Nevertheless, there is concern that the flagging competitive status of U.S. firms in "upstream" hardware manufacturing industries, particularly semiconductor manufacturing equipment and certain segments of the semiconductor industry, could place the U.S. systems integration industry at a disadvantage in international markets. Foreign firms with strengths in these building-block industries, such as the Japanese firms mentioned above, could leverage their technological advantages in the expanding market for computer and communications networks, especially if U.S. systems integration firms do not have timely access to new hardware products.

Sources of U.S. Advantage

U.S. leadership in systems integration is attributed to a variety of factors, some more tangible than others. An acknowledged source of advantage is the continuing strong performance of the U.S. software manufacturers, who account for more than 60 percent of the global market. Software, particularly customized programs, is the primary source of the "value-added or content of the systems we build," explained Samuel H. Fuller, Digital Equipment Corporation's vice president for research. Virtually all colloquium participants agreed that maintaining the U.S. advantage in software design and development is critical to future success in the emerging global market for systems integration services.

"Ultimately," said Alfred V. Aho, assistant vice president at Bell Communications Research, "software is going to be the limiting factor" in determining the value and utility of integrated systems, as well as the success of firms vying to build these systems.

Also important but often unappreciated, according to several speakers, is the advantage conferred by international acceptance of many computer and communications standards that originated in the United States. This conformance with U.S. standards reflects in large part the nation's pioneering role in developing and applying information technology, resulting in a kind of after-the-fact acceptance of proven technologies. International adoption of technology developed in the United States opened world markets to U.S. firms and obliged local competitors to follow the U.S. lead.

However, international standards organizations are becoming much more proactive and are attempting to anticipate technological progress. Their aim is to integrate important innovations into standards as new technology nears commercial application, avoiding the ferment of de facto standardization and providing information-technology users with an efficient means of linking existing and new hardware and software. In practice, international standards bodies have far to go to achieve this model of efficiency, but proactive approaches significantly enhance the strategic importance of standards making. Firms that are the most adept in the standards arena may be able to leapfrog the current competition when new generations of computing and communication technology are ready for the marketplace. In the opinion of some colloquium participants, U.S. firms and the federal government have been far more passive than their European and Japanese counterparts in international standards-setting activities that are likely to shape the future of information networks.

The success of U.S. systems integration firms may also stem from what a number of colloquium speakers described as an American capacity for flexible thinking and managing complexity, a hallmark of integrated information systems. Irving Wladawsky-Berger, assistant general manager of development and quality for IBM's Enterprise Systems, emphasized that the nation's prowess in design and innovation and its propensity for change helped stake the U.S. industry to its leadership position. Selin expressed a similar view. "As long as our computer industry concentrates on building applications and building problem-solving systems and not just trying to produce chips or simple devices in larger numbers and more cheaply than other people do, I think we'll do very well," he said.

But the complexity wrought by an ever-growing web of interconnected technologies, people, and organizations has also led to efforts to create order and simplicity. Standards are one manifestation of these efforts (see Chapter 3 appendix, "Standards Making at a Glance"). For example, the evolving standard for Integrated Services Digital Network (ISDN) service promises to provide an interface for worldwide networking. Growing interest in object-oriented programming and in reusable software elements is another illustration of efforts to simplify systems integration and eliminate some of the complexity and redundancy in building information networks.

Within these emerging areas, cautioned Wladawsky-Berger, may lie the seeds of problems for U.S. systems integration firms. "Executing well is absolutely paramount," he said. "It may be that the design part of systems integration, which is where we excel, is becoming an ever-smaller part of the total problem, and the execution part of it—that is, 'get the damn thing built and working'—is where more and more of the problems are. Now, notice that, while we in the United States are superb in this ferment of design and innovation, lots has been written about our weaknesses in the back end, in executing. . . . That is something I think we need to watch out for."

Selin noted, however, that greater standardization and uniformity in applications would likely create more opportunities, at both the low and high ends of the market. With increasing standardization, he said, "the detailed specification of the components becomes less important. . . . What happens is that for problems that took a one-of-a-kind solution, where everything was customized and therefore so expensive that very few companies could afford to solve their problems, it now becomes feasible to do three-quarters of the software with an applications-specific piece of software. Therefore," he continued, "you make it economical for a much larger range of companies to come in. . . . [T]he total size of the market will increase considerably because more and more organizations will be able to afford what only a few could before. At the same time, you go out and you do tougher things."

As technology and skills improve, Selin added, systems integrators will be called on to solve "one-of-a-kind problems that are more complex than anything we thought possible 10 years ago."

CONVERGING TECHNOLOGY: A DRIVING FORCE

A common base of digital technology is evolving rapidly. The computer now exists in many forms—from supercomputers and massively parallel machines to the ubiquitous desk-top and lap-top personal computers to the highly portable pen-based and palm-top computers that are now emerging. Just as significant as this diversity is the tremendous variety of complementing devices for communicating, gathering, and presenting information. Besides the familiar printer, the "peripheral" devices of computers now include copiers, facsimile machines, telephones, answering machines, pagers, scanners, electronic cameras, data-storage devices, optical and electronic sensors, and a vast and growing array of computer-controlled machinery.

Although the decade-old prediction of a personal computer in every home is not even close to being realized, digitally controlled devices with embedded software and hardware are pervasive in the home: video cassette recorders and cameras, compact disc players, telephones, microwaves, and other appliances. In prospect is an all-digital high-definition television system, a development that could transform that most ubiquitous and passive of household appliances into a machine capable of storing, retrieving, and manipulating video images.

The convergence of technologies is also evident in the area of wireless communications, now principally the domain of cellular telephones. Several firms have developed wireless methods for linking computers in networks. Such over-the-air connections between computers will make network configurations as flexible as those for cellular telephones.

As the communication capabilities of computers grow and as communication devices become more computerlike, opportunities for information services and products multiply. The hybridization of information technology blurs distinctions between industries, giving rise to rivalries among firms that once competed in separate markets. For consumers, the ubiquity of digital technology creates exciting new opportunities—new ways to gather and manipulate information, new ways to work and recreate, and new ways to collaborate. For businesses, the technology creates new opportunities that extend throughout and across organizations. Many firms are now seeking to achieve the synergies afforded by information networking through systems integration.

Today, however, systems integration is an option largely restricted to large firms, some of which have invested over $1 billion to revamp their corporate information systems and create an infrastructure for distributed computing networks. Such high costs attest to the complexity and the magnitude of the task. The expense and complexity also reflect the difficulties posed by the lack of standards and communication protocols essential for networks linking a heterogeneous collection of equipment. As a result, many of today's networks do not achieve the ideal of a seamless computing and communications environment. Each brand of equipment may have its own control computer, and even the most vigilant network management teams can have trouble isolating and responding to problems that can disrupt the entire information system. The potential for problems is magnified, and new ones, such as the threat of security breaches, arise when organizations link their private networks to those of other organizations or when network access can be achieved through public telephone lines.

A NETWORKED SOCIETY: ISSUES AND CHALLENGES

As ambitious as they are, today's systems integration projects are microcosms of the nation- and globe-spanning information networks that are expected to evolve. In effect, said Robert L. Martin, vice president for software technology and systems at Bell Communications Research, the benefits now being reaped by firms that have invested in their own information networks would be extended to small businesses and individuals. "You could bring intelligence further down the economic hierarchy," he added.

Visions of the computer age's more revolutionary successor, the information age, cast the computer as a gateway that provides access to information in virtually all parts of the world. Proponents of the information-age equivalent to universal telephone access contend that a national information infrastructure is vital to the nation's economic competitiveness.

"I believe the broader issue is to change the concept of a system to a highly networked distributed base," Martin said. "You would then have an education network that could bring the appropriate educational talent to the disabled, the gifted, or the average student. You would have a very different form of health system."

Such thinking is not confined to the United States. In Europe and Japan, government and industry are funding collaborative research and development projects to address the technological hurdles that must be overcome to develop an infrastructure and the services it would support. The Japanese and European governments are also fostering development of key standards for achieving compatibility and interoperability. Several European nations have implemented accelerated schedules for installing the digital networks and common channel signaling necessary for ISDN service. In Japan, the Nippon Telephone and Telegraph Co. has announced its intention to develop the most advanced telecommunications system in the world. By 1995, it intends to offer ISDN service in all 56 Japanese cities, and by the year 2015, it will link all homes by optical fiber.[8] At the same time, Japan's Ministry of International Trade and Industry (MITI) has initiated a series of programs designed to integrate its computer, telecommunications, and other information-related industries and to network its society. Recently announced initiatives include research and development projects on interoperable database systems and improved graphical user interfaces, modeling studies of "information age cities," and several cooperative research programs aimed at helping developing countries build their own information networks.[9]

Colloquium participants did not see U.S. government and industry as attending to the nation's information infrastructure with the same levels of determination and comprehensiveness as those exhibited in Japan and Europe. Virtually all endorsed administration and legislative proposals calling for the creation of a National Research and Education Network (NREN), an information "superhighway" that eventually would transmit data at rates of several billion bits per second, or more than 1,000 times faster than today's standard data networks. As proposed, NREN would connect the nation's universities and collaborating companies. The administration's initiative, called the High Performance Computing and Communications (HPCC) program, would provide a focal point for developing the hardware, software, and systems that a truly national information infrastructure will require. (See Chapter 4 for a discussion of the HPCC program.)

Indeed, whether practiced on the scale of a single company or on the scale of an entire nation, systems integration poses a variety of technical, social, economic, and regulatory issues, which are examined in the next chapters.

NOTES

1. Dorros, Irwin. 1990. "Calling for Cooperation," *Bellcore Exchange*, November-December, p. 7.

2. For example, 18 midsize paper companies with collective annual revenues of $4 billion pooled their resources to create a $50 million global information network that links the companies, offices of major customers, and international sales offices. This system permits same-day responses to inquiries from customers, as compared with the industry average of 12 days. (Konsynski, Benn R., and F. Warren McFarlan. 1990. "Information Partnerships—Shared Data, Shared Scale," *Harvard Business Review*, September-October, pp. 115-118.)

Also, a number of Wall Street security firms—where information technology expenditures can account for 15 percent to 20 percent of expenses—are engaged in several types of cooperative activities, including sharing disaster-recovery sites, combining and distributing their analytical libraries, and developing a shared Electronic Data Interchange network. (Ambrosio, Johanna. 1991. "Wall Street Firms Try Shared Technology," *ComputerWorld*, June 24.)

3. Computer Science and Technology Board, National Research Council. 1988. *The National Challenge in Computer Science and Technology*, National Academy Press, Washington, D.C. See also the September 1991 issue of *Scientific American*, which has several articles relating to information infrastructure.

4. Department of Commerce. 1991. *U.S. Industrial Outlook 1991*, Information Services, Government Printing Office, Washington D.C., p. 27-5.

5. As reported in Gartner Group Inc. 1990. "Systems Integration Scenario," Gartner Group Inc., Greenwich, Conn., p. 7.

6. Rothfeder, Jeffrey, Peter Coy, and Gary McWilliams. 1990. "Taming the Wild Network," *Business Week*, October 8, p. 143.

7. Shapiro, Eben. 1991. "AT&T Buying Computer Maker in Stock Deal Worth $7.4 Billion," *New York Times*, May 7, p. A1.

8. Bellcore Technical Liaison Office. 1990. "Japanese Telecommunications," unpublished paper, Bellcore, Morristown, N.J., July, p. 2-1.

9. For a compelling discussion of the enormous potential for an information infrastructure to transform society as seen by Japan's Ministry of International Trade and Industry (MITI), the reader is referred to the so-called "Sixth Generation" or New Information Processing Technology (NIPT) project currently proposed by MITI and discussed in its *Report of the Research Committee on New Information Processing Technology*, Industrial Electronics Division, Machinery and Information Industries Bureau, Ministry of International Trade and Industry, March 1991.

2

Applications of Integrated Systems: Evolution in Concept and Practice

Ask a dozen practitioners what systems integration is, and you will probably get as many different definitions (see Box 2.1). Ask that same group what systems integration is intended to accomplish, and the answers are likely to be more uniform. The standard response is "solutions" or "application solutions." For people who are not steeped in the field, however, that answer prompts a fundamental question: What's the problem in the first place?

Typically, the set of needs and problems that an integrated computing and communications system addresses is unique to an organization. At snack food maker Frito-Lay, for example, the challenge was to develop an information system that helped the company leverage the advantages and efficiencies that accrue to its large size and yet enabled the national firm to maneuver flexibly in local markets, where it sells the 5 billion packages of snack food that generate annual revenue of $4.5 billion. The company's integrated system, widely used as an example of an effective corporate information system, links all parts of its operations. The system has allowed Frito-Lay "to be decentralized in its marketplace activities," explained Charles S. Feld, vice president for management information systems, "and at the same time, leverage our whole manufacturing and logistics system. We have been able to do that through the use of information and technology, primarily by providing information to the people that have to make decisions lower in the organization." (See Box 2.2.)

MOTIVATIONS FOR SYSTEMS INTEGRATION

Despite the great variability in the issues and needs organizations seek to resolve with applications of information technology, there are at least five general categories of motivations for investing in systems integration.

Box 2.1. Definitions of Systems Integration

"Fulfilling a practical objective through the assemblage of diverse component technologies and disciplines that are critical to each other's success. It is a teaming of technology components that results in high synergy."

—Jeffrey M. Heller, *Senior Vice President, Electronic Data Systems*

Systems integration is "process innovation—to simplify basic business operations, to compress the time they require, and to narrow the gap between the product or service and the customer."

—W. James Fischer, *Managing Partner, Andersen Consulting*

"People building upon existing components to satisfy a customer's need."

—Robert L. Martin, *Vice President for Software Technology and Systems, Bell Communications Research*

"Effective integration implies a system-level architecture that permits the integration, or connection, of system components and permits later integration of unplanned components. Effective integration also implies an integrating mechanism that permits components to share data. It implies an overall model that permits the user to understand what the system is doing. It implies a constant user interface. It also requires integration of the functions of the applications that the system supports."

—Larry E. Druffel, *Director, Software Engineering Institute, Carnegie Mellon University*

"It started with technology—putting bits and pieces together—and grew into managing information. It has grown into understanding processes and now, I believe, it is getting into understanding the human element of what we are trying to accomplish."

—Michael Taylor, *Central Systems Engineering Manager, Digital Equipment Corporation*

"Solving a problem efficiently, recursively; giving disparate components a single-system look and feel. . . We should keep [integrated information systems] simple so that we can maintain them and use them, and we should keep them affordable so they will deliver the greatest value to the largest number of people."

—Alfred V. Aho, *Assistant Vice President, Bell Communications Research*

Box 2.2.   The Frito-Lay Information System

If an executive at Frito-Lay headquarters near Dallas wants to know how his company's products are faring on supermarket shelves in Boston, or the price of a corn futures contract at the Chicago Board of Trade, or the fuel efficiency of the company's delivery fleet, that information is instantly available. In fact, current information on virtually every aspect of the snack food maker's operations—manufacturing, purchasing, warehousing, distribution, marketing, sales, management, and research—is easily retrieved with the company's information system and presented in the level of detail desired.

Widely cited as a model of an effective corporate information system, Frito-Lay's computer network has established itself as the company's most important strategic and competitive tool. Executives say it is a requirement for business survival in the 1990s.

A national company competing against local and regional snack food manufacturers for shelf and display space in more than 400,000 stores, the subsidiary of Pepsico Inc. has used its comprehensive intelligence to transform itself into a "micromarketer" that enjoys the economies of scale that accrue to a multibillion-dollar enterprise.

"We learned how to handle the volume, we learned how to handle the speed over the years," explained Charles S. Feld, Frito-Lay's vice president for management information systems. "But what has happened to us is, our marketplace has gotten very complex. Boston is now very different from Chicago, very different from California; supermarkets are different from convenience stores; and products are differentiated by flavors and bag sizes. The world is no longer one size or one color of jeans. Everybody wants diversity. So we have had to figure out a way to leverage our size and prowess in the marketplace and still be able to compete on a very targeted basis."

The company's 10,000-person sales force provides the information that is key to Frito-Lay's nimble performance in local markets. Equipped with handheld computers, a sales person keys in orders during sales calls and furnishes customers with a printout, an on-the-spot sales receipt with tax, discounts, and promotions included. At the end of each day, the sales force electronically transmits sales, orders, and other information to the headquarter's mainframe computer. The next morning, the sales people link up again with the mainframe to receive the day's routing and scheduling information.

With the daily-updated information from the field, the company can track performance in precise detail, down to the sales movement of an individual product in a single store. As a result, managers say they know more about local marketing conditions than their competitors do, and they can devise sales strategies accordingly.

Before the networked information system was introduced, the company's marketing strategy consisted of two or three national initiatives, formulated at the top of the organization. Now, with the benefit of detailed knowledge of local markets, middle managers generate and execute some 300 sales-building ideas each year. While top management oversees these local and regional marketing initiatives, the shift in tactical responsibilities permits executives to focus more on the company's strategic direction.

Executives at the 60-year-old company, which employs 26,000 people, cite effective teamwork across the organization as the primary advantage of the information system. Benefits have been realized in many forms. Electronic data entry by the sales force eliminated time-consuming paperwork, saving between 30,000 and 50,000 hours each week. The company was able to consolidate 400 sales routes even as its annual sales volume increased to $4.5 billion, from $3.7 billion. Improved tracking of product movement reduced the number of "stales" (products that have exceeded their shelf lives) from 2 percent of sales volume to less than 1 percent, resulting in annual savings of $39 million.

Designed to accommodate changing needs and new applications, the information system continues to evolve and increase its strategic and operational value to the company.

Feld attributes the success of the system to three enabling factors: "a business proposition worthy of the investment" in information technology, systems integration skill, and "the will to see the job through during tough times."

1. *For many organizations, experiences with information technology have not lived up to expectations.* American business invested billions in computing and communications technology during the 1980s.[1] At the start of the decade, the nation's inventory of computer terminals totaled about 4 million; as of today, some 75 million IBM-compatible personal computers alone have been sold, and half of all U.S. office workers have a computer on their desks.[2] Many firms realized significant benefits. But a large number did not, or at least returns to their investments were not commensurate with initial expectations. One major disappointment was the negligible improvement in the productivity of the service sector (although gains were made in the quality and diversity of service output), which has been estimated to account for about 85 percent of the nation's total stock of information technology items.[3]

Hindsight offers some valuable lessons. The most obvious, of course, is that merely possessing technology, regardless of its capabilities, does not translate automatically into an organizational asset. As simple as it may seem now, this lesson is actually the product of evolutionary changes in technology and, most important, in understanding the role of that technology.

2. *The proliferation of information technology products and vendors has produced the need for connectivity and interoperability.* Many organizations own heterogeneous collections of computing and communication equipment, purchasing, for example, one vendor's machines for engineers, another's for administrative support staff, and yet another's for managing large databases and on-line transaction-processing activities. Because of incompatibilities in operating systems and other vendor-specific peculiarities, dissimilar machines, and the people who used them, functioned in isolation. Exchanging information between these computing islands entailed laborious translation procedures or, worse yet, manual reentry of information.

This state of affairs led to user demand for connectivity, a means to let unlike systems perform at least rudimentary tasks such as exchanging files. But connectivity was not enough. Users also wanted their hardware and software to be interoperable, that is, to make applications, information, and peripheral devices easily accessible to any computer, regardless of who made it and what operating system it used.

3. *An installed base of information technology has to accommodate new technology and new capabilities.* The need to combine the old with the new is a perennial source of headaches for managers of information systems. Firms that have invested vast sums in information technology cannot simply jettison that investment and start anew with each successive wave of commercial innovation. Nor would they want to even if they could afford it. The databases and applications embedded within existing information systems are often described as the "corporate jewels," strategically important assets that are integrally related to the firms' operations. Moreover, the value of existing information and programs can be increased greatly when integrated with the capabilities of new hardware and software.

4. *Advances in technology, combined with growing appreciation of what can be accomplished with that technology, have prompted firms to search for new applications and sources of competitive advantage.* Although the computer—or, more appropriately, the ever-growing family of digital technologies—may not yet merit the title of universal machine, growing appreciation of its potential is inspiring organizations to apply the technology in new ways and, in so doing, pursue new business opportunities. Just as important, new capabilities in computing and communications are motivating individual firms and groups of firms—suppliers and customers and even industries—to reevaluate their entire way of doing business.

5. *In an increasingly global economy, firms must rely on telecommunications and information technology to manage and coordinate their operations and to stay abreast of international competitors.* The ability to communicate and transmit large volumes of data nearly instantaneously facilitates closer linkages with foreign subsidiaries, suppliers, and customers, but it also telescopes the time organizations have to respond to changes in international markets and to the actions of competitors. If, for example, a manufacturing firm's competitors can place electronic orders with foreign suppliers or change the specifications for a part and transmit the new design immediately to a collaborator located half the world away, then that firm must also have the same capabilities just to keep pace with the competition.

None of these motivations stands entirely apart from the others. Collectively, they are driving businesses and other organizations to use their information technology innovatively and effectively. Moreover, information networking technology is so intricately related to the broader phenomenon of the growing interdependency among regional, national, and global economies that the importance of its role can only be expected to increase.

DISTRIBUTED NETWORKED COMPUTING: EVOLUTION IN UNDERSTANDING

The steady stream of complementing innovations in computer and communications technology provides the building blocks of systems integration projects. Components of hardware and software are integrated into distributed computing networks, which many firms view as their "central nervous systems," the means to coordinate all elements of their operations into a synergistic whole. The result is a sprouting of electronic and optical-fiber connections that link the information age's equivalents to the pools of neurons of varying size and function that make up the central nervous system and work in concert with the brain. Centers of activity range from individual computers on a network to local area networks (LANs), which connect computers at single sites, to wide area networks (WANs) that link LANs or individual machines across a region, a nation, or the world.

While networks of machines and devices are the ostensible manifestations of the trend toward distributed computing and communications, the most significant connections, according to colloquium participants, are those between people and organizational units using linked devices. It is at the level of the worker that systems integration and distributed computing should have its greatest impact, many asserted.

This expectation is markedly different from the notions of automation that have heavily influenced computer applications since the 1960s. In the early days of commercial computing, companies used the technology to automate "simple stand-alone processes," explained Gerard R. Weis, senior vice president at Sears Technology Services Inc. "We would do things like capture data, keypunch it, and report on it simply to compress the time from the time we got the data until we produced a report and to obtain operational cost savings by reducing the number of people who manually produced those reports."

In the following decade, according to the recounting of Weis and other participants, firms began to link automated processes within some units of their business. The result was what has been described as archipelagos of automation created from islands of automation.

"The 1980s," said Weis, drawing on his own company's experiences, "saw us take two divergent paths. . . . On the business side, we focused on data integration and data-based management so that we began to tie together information in the various lines of businesses. On the technology side, we focused on pushing down the cost of running those systems and on making sure that the infrastructure would support the data integration that was going on at the applications level."

What many firms have learned during this 30-year evolution is that automating business as usual did not tap the most significant competitive advantages that can be achieved with information technology, explained W. James Fischer, managing partner for technology services at Andersen Consulting. Whatever the gains inherent in this approach of assigning computing technology to its most obvious uses—preparing payrolls, budgets, and inventories and performing other number-crunching tasks—they were likely to be short-lived advantages because such applications are readily available to all competitors, he said.

In contrast to the past pattern of responding incrementally and, often, in piecemeal fashion to the growing capabilities of information technology, firms in the current decade may use the technology to redefine themselves. That is what Weis foresees happening at Sears. "[W]e have to reassess our business processes and our culture," he said, "and figure out then how to make the business run differently and to exploit technology in fostering that change."

SYSTEMS INTEGRATION AS "PROCESS INNOVATION"

Structural and cultural change is a formidable challenge for any firm, public agency, or other type of organization. Yet for most organizations, maintaining the status quo will likely mean that they will not realize the most significant advantages afforded by the technology, contended Fischer, whose responsibilities at Andersen Consulting include devising a comprehensive firm-wide view for applying information technology.

"[S]ystems integration," he said, "really ought to be about the business of process innovation," which, by definition, necessitates change. Process innovation entails changing the ways companies "perform their standard business functions, changing the way they manufacture, changing the way they distribute, changing the way their orders are taken, and changing the way they sell their product," he explained.

Ultimately, Fischer said, the aim is to "simplify the business": to reduce the time it takes to perform key activities and to narrow the gaps between the personnel and the functions that support those activities. Within manufacturing firms, this requires erasing barriers between design, engineering, production, marketing, and distribution. Fischer also maintained that the new cooperative links forged by systems integration should extend outside the organization and tighten relationships with suppliers and customers.

Mark Teflian, vice president and chief information officer at Covia, which operates the world's second-largest computerized airline reservation system, offered a different yet complementary conceptual framework for appraising the transformational role of networked information technology. Global competition and the rapid diffusion of technology across international borders, he said, have shortened the competitive life of most products and, consequently, collapsed the time a firm has to recover costs and generate profits that support succeeding cycles of innovation and product introductions. Increasingly, Teflian predicted, firms will regard their products as perishable products with limited shelf lives. Seizing short-lived marketing opportunities and optimizing pricing strategies will require timely capture of information at the point of sale and rapid response to changing market conditions.

The growing value of timely information, Teflian asserted, will spur wide adoption of on-line transaction-processing (OLTP) systems. Pioneered by airlines that developed computerized reservation systems, OLTP systems provide computer users on a network with simultaneous real-time access to shared databases. Whenever necessary, users can retrieve information, change it, and enter new information, thereby updating the databases and providing others on the network with the most current information available. According to Teflian, such on-line systems offer firms the means to broaden and deepen their intelligence, a fundamental requirement for rapid and informed decision making.

ASSIMILATING INFORMATION AND ENABLING PEOPLE

As customers, software and hardware manufacturers, and system integrators reassess the roles and uses of information technology, people emerge as the most critical element and as the element most resistant to the organizational changes that systems integration fosters. Integrating people—helping them assimilate information, create, collaborate, and, in sum, work more productively—is the highest-order task of systems integration. Ulti-mately, the success or failure of systems integration is determined not by "groups of technology," Teflian contended, but by how effectively networks help people "process and assimilate information." Overcoming incompatibili-ties between computer operating systems and other systems-engineering hurdles are "minor problems," he said, compared with the challenge of adapting the technology to ensure that it is truly an enabling tool for the people who use it.

Systems integrators and their customers have devoted most of their atten-tion to technical issues, which, obviously, if not resolved will impede effec-tive use of information technology. But such issues should not obscure the fact that the true measure of information technology's value is its impact on human and organizational performance, advised Max Hopper, American Air-lines senior vice president for information systems. To illustrate his point, Hopper offered as an example his company's collaboration with the French national railroad to develop a computer reservation system, called Reserv-rail. Through the systems integration project, the railroad is taking a 20-year "leap" in technology, he said, but the physical deployment of the enabl-ing computer and communications equipment represents only a secondary part of the process. "I do not think it is a piece of hardware," he explained. "I mean, it did not make a damn bit of difference whether the computer that is used is a PC [personal computer] or a supercomputer. It . . . really relates to changing the way the company does business. That is where, I think, there is skill [needed]."

That skill, however, is at a nascent stage of development. "I think we are just starting to understand the fact that the computing system has to be driven by the human system," said Michael Taylor, central systems engi-neering manager at the Digital Equipment Corp. "We are starting to think in terms of a new paradigm that says you start with the people, the way those people need to do work. Forget all this technology. That will come later. But look at the people, look at what those people have to do, and see what you can do to make them more productive."

With this perspective on using information technology to make workers more effective, the purview of systems integration expands greatly. Into a domain largely devoted to solving detailed technical problems enter issues intricately related to cultural notions of work. For example, networking is expected to enable greater cooperation and interaction among workers, but it is not at all clear how to foster a truly collaborative, computer-supported work style and to capture the anticipated productivity benefits.

ACHIEVING EFFECTIVE SYSTEMS INTEGRATION

Faced with a task of such breadth and complexity, systems integrators and their customers may be tempted to dissect the economic, technological, organizational, and cultural problems and issues they confront into ever-smaller parts. But Feld of Frito-Lay warned against this tendency. "We need to think about [information systems]," he said, "in much longer time frames and from a much higher mountain. . . . Breaking down the problem to smaller elements is going in the wrong direction because you cannot see what is happening. You have got to be able to step above it" and view the system as a whole.

Yet, the whole is a composite creation—a one-of-a-kind assembly of many people and many individual pieces of hardware and software—built by interdisciplinary and often geographically separated teams. Coordination is essential and difficult. In such a complex undertaking, the system-wide perspective that Feld advocated can easily be lost. Moreover, methodological tools to guide systems integration projects and help ensure congruence and complementarity among supporting tasks and products are at a rudimentary stage. In fact, colloquium participants generally agreed that building large integrated systems from heterogeneous collections of hardware and software remains more an imperfect art than a structured scientific or engineering discipline.

Numerous pitfalls are inherent in the process and, consequently, it is not uncommon for an information system to fall short of expectations held at the beginning of a systems integration project. For example, more than a few anecdotal accounts describe projects that greatly exceeded their budget or, worse yet, were abandoned after considerable investments of money and time. Consider the experiences of the federal government, the largest user of systems integration services. In 1990 the General Accounting Office reported that the government spends $20 billion annually to improve its 53,000 computer systems. But the watchdog agency found that "attempts to modernize the government's information systems have produced few successes and many costly failures."[4]

In addition, problems arise after information systems are up and running. Equipment problems, programming errors, and other disruptive events cause network failures, resulting in annual losses estimated to range from $600,000 to $3 million for firms with large systems.[5,6] Moreover, unauthorized use of networks and other security abuses have resulted in large, but untabulated, losses of money and information.[7]

Acknowledging the difficulties and complexities that can undermine the aims of system integration, colloquium participants identified some of the key attributes of efforts to build effective information systems, as well as the essential features of those systems.

Understanding the Organization and the Application Area

From the various definitions of systems integration offered by participants, one might deduce that effectiveness is variously perceived by the beholders—the organizations and people who will use the information system. For example, Jeffrey M. Heller, senior vice president at Electronic Data Systems, described an effective systems integration project as one that fulfills a "practical objective through the assemblage of diverse component technologies and disciplines that are critical to each others' success." At a general level, this definition seems straightforward enough, but it can become exceedingly complex at the operational level of an individual organization. "The formulation of customer requirements," Heller said, may be the most important and least appreciated aspect of systems integration. Added Feld of Frito-Lay, "You have to have a business proposition that is worthy of the investment" in an integrated system of information technology.

Translating a business plan into an integrated set of hardware, databases, and applications, according to Fischer of Andersen Consulting, requires an approach that encompasses each of the main elements common to every company: the overriding business strategy, the technology and the operations supporting that strategy, and the skill levels of the work force. "These four elements must be synchronized, or important synergies will be lost," Fischer said. "If any of you had the opportunity to review systems that were designed in the past 20 years, you would find that none of them reflects an understanding of all four elements."

An essential element of this understanding, according to several participants, is comprehensive knowledge of the particular attributes of the industry in which a client company is competing and of the unique characteristics of that customer's business. Customized applications developed without this knowledge are not likely to satisfy a customer's information needs, nor to provide the competitive advantages that the firm was seeking from its investment in technology. For U.S. systems integration firms aiming to compete in foreign markets, advised Ivan Selin, thorough familiarity with the application area as practiced in target countries may be the most important determinant of exporting success. (See Box 2.3.)

Increasingly, integrators are recognizing the need to be intimately familiar with application areas, a recognition that has motivated strategic partnerships with consulting organizations expert in the strategic issues of a particular industry. In addition, there is growing appreciation of the multidisciplinary nature of systems integration and the concomitant need for collaborative teamwork throughout the development process. The need for expertise in computers, software, communications, and the application domain remains critical. But some integrators are choosing to broaden their perspective and are now augmenting their teams with anthropologists, social scientists, and other specialists who can, for example, address issues related to the design of user interfaces and to how people adjust to collaborative work environments.

Box 2.3 Thoughts on Exporting

Systems integration has the "makings of a great export industry," Ivan Selin, then under secretary for management in the U.S. State Department (he is now chairman of the Nuclear Regulatory Commission), told the colloquium. For U.S. firms to preserve and build on their commanding position in the emerging international market, Selin emphasized, they must execute a lesson already learned in the domestic market: To build effective integrated information systems, firms must be intimately familiar with the characteristics of the foreign industries and companies they are working with. He expanded on this point:

> First, of course, are the obstacles to any kind of high-technology export. You have to know the language, you need entree to the customers, you may need local partners, [and so on]. . . . Then there are some additional obstacles specific to integrated systems. First of all, by definition, we're talking about major applications. We're talking about a lot of time, a lot of effort, a lot of customized software, a lot of industry-specific standard software, and a lot of hardware. Before you can sell one of these major applications you really need to know the industry as practiced in the target country, not just as practiced in the United States. Depending on the industry, there are major differences from country to country.
>
> But you also need to know the company, because, again, these are not products off the shelf; they're specific to a particular company's applications, and these are hard to know. Even if you devote a lot of time and effort to understand international banking or, say, trade documentation, when you go to Japan you find out that documents are done differently from the way they are done in the United States. The companies are different, the culture is different, what they are willing to share from one company to another is different. . . .
>
> On top of that, . . . you are talking about doing applications that are deeply involved in the "innards" of how the company operates, and so companies tend to be very reluctant to bring in outside firms to do really mainline systems. It's one thing to buy something off the shelf or out of a catalogue; it's another to trust an outsider to come in and develop a system that will be central to the operation of that company for a long time to come. On the one hand, the company is terribly dependent on the outsider to provide the system successfully; on the other hand, that outsider is going to walk away with a lot of inside information, and in many societies and many companies that is something that is given up very reluctantly. Finally, you need to have experts in the country to which you are exporting. It's not enough to have very good sales representatives and very good maintenance people—you need to have the people who have a fair share of the information that was necessary to develop the system in the first place.

"To be successful," said Albert B. Crawford, executive vice president for strategic business systems at American Express Travel Related Services, "a systems integration contractor must demonstrate relevant experience in multiple disciplines and in successfully managing extremely large, complex projects." However, finding people with the requisite mix of skills to achieve that level of performance is becoming increasingly difficult for the systems integration industry.

Recognizing Essential Features of Information Systems

System Architecture

The rapid advance of computer and communications technology underlies an ever-changing set of user needs. New capabilities create new business opportunities and, at the same time, open the door to new competition, necessitating a change in business strategies and operations and, consequently, in the information systems on which firms depend. As a result, businesses want to be able to capitalize on new technology offerings, but without having to start from scratch with each new round of innovation or each newly identified information need.

Thus a key attribute of an integrated information system is flexibility, the ability to evolve to accommodate unforeseen technologies and information needs and to be adapted with relative ease to address new competitive challenges. Such flexibility, however, has not been a hallmark of information systems.

In the past, said Taylor of the Digital Equipment Corp., integrators "created some very innovative, very creative, very unique solutions to the business problems of the era. The bad news was that with this very creativeness and uniqueness, we caused difficulties. . . . Companies [now] looking at these integrated solutions of a few years ago find that, because they are unique, they are difficult to migrate forward, they are difficult to evolve as the underlying technology changes, and what, at the time, was a competitive advantage for the firm could well become a competitive disadvantage if indeed that solution is rigid and inflexible and geared to a way of doing business that is no longer in tune with the way that corporation now wants to do business."

These experiences point to the need for a consistent systems architecture assembled with modular building blocks—hardware, software, database, and communications platforms with flexible linkages, or interfaces. Standardization and the move toward open systems are yielding modular products that, in effect, can be bolted on or plugged into existing systems and yet are malleable enough to link to tomorrow's technology.

"From a technology perspective," Taylor explained, "we are taking a much more architectural approach. That says you need building blocks, you need to innovate within those building blocks but you need to retain that architectural framework so that the whole evolution is not impeded by the fact that everything is interconnected to everything else."

The growth of information networking, however, has outpaced standards development and the computer industry's migration to open systems. Many organizations that are pioneering applications of information technology still bear the risk of being locked into proprietary systems that may restrict future options for connectivity and interoperability.[8] For now, these organizations must choose from among competing platforms, hoping that their selections will become the nationally and internationally accepted and implemented standards.

If a firm is large enough, it can try to dictate its architectural requirements to prospective suppliers, as American Express Travel Related Services has done in the area of communication components. According to Crawford, who oversees development of the subsidiary's global information system, American Express has stipulated a set of standard interfaces that equipment suppliers must provide.

American Express, like many other firms, is now endeavoring to build an underlying architecture for its global information system, a framework on which to combine old and new technology and build coherent solutions rather than a patchwork of partial solutions. Like a well-conceived plan that includes contingencies for uncertainty, a good systems architecture is expansive and adaptable. But, Crawford explained, it also exerts controls to ensure that new equipment, databases, and applications achieve the desired levels of connectivity and interoperability.

Frito-Lay's new corporate information system provides an example of the benefits that accrue to an architecture that can evolve with changing needs. "One of the fundamental design criteria" in Frito-Lay's layered architecture, explained Feld, who directed the development of the company's system, is the ability to accommodate change. For example, only minor database adjustments are required if the firm revamps its employee pay structures or even if it restructures the organization. "We have 32 areas of the country now," Feld said. "If we wanted to drop down to 28, it is a weekend database reorganization." Because of the disaggregated nature of the information system, major alterations in one area do not generate unwanted and unforeseen changes in others, he explained.

Data Communication Capabilities

Because of heavy network and internetwork traffic or because of their need for specialized computing and communication capabilities, such as the transmission of large graphics files, firms are paying as much attention to their data-transmission capabilities and information-retrieval times as they are to such perennial issues as processing power and memory and storage capacity. Some have invested in building private information infrastructures, often at considerable expense. For example, when General Motors (GM) initiated its massive program to automate its manufacturing operations, about half of its outlays for computer systems went for communications-related equipment and software.[9] Today, corporate spending for private networks accounts for more than half of all spending for communications networks in the United States.[10]

But in building their high-speed networks, firms are entering into murky waters. The unsettled state of high-level communications protocols necessary for exchanging information and applications within and between networks means today's choices could complicate efforts to satisfy tomorrow's networking needs if alternative conventions emerge as the industry standards. Moreover, even the largest firms are discovering that, as the trend to internetworking and interenterprise cooperation proceeds, they can no longer entirely bypass public telecommunications carriers, an amalgam of international, national, regional, and local utilities, or the growing number of third-party suppliers of enhanced telecommunications and information services. This increases the number of interfaces and, therefore, potential bottlenecks that must be negotiated for internetworking applications, while increasing the vulnerability of a firm's communications and information system to security violations and technical failures.

Security

As internetworking grows, the potential for theft of data, other security abuses, and accidents also increases. For example, technical problems in one network can cause deterioration of service in connected networks. Internal safeguards developed by managers of private networks will no longer suffice, but effective responses to new risks have yet to be developed.

"Five years ago," explained Weis of Sears, "we were less concerned about the outside world, and we had pretty good security means that we could implement privately within the company." But today, as Sears makes greater use of public voice and data communication networks, its information system has become more vulnerable, he said—"There are some policy issues that need to be resolved." For example, automatic number identification, which provides the telephone number of a person who gains access to an information system by means of a modem, would permit managers to audit usage. The technology, however, has raised privacy issues that have resulted in lawsuits.

Better security, said Fischer of Andersen Consulting, is "an extremely severe challenge for the future." With more and more companies billing, ordering, and handling other tasks through electronic data interchange (EDI) and as electronic links to consumers increase, he added, "You can see how the possibilities for security violations go up exponentially. So it is a problem that we see as very, very key for the future of the industry."

Network Management and Reliability

"Nobody has yet given us the capable tools for network management of the scale, type, and variety that we need," complained Crawford of American Express. As a result, American Express, in collaboration with IBM, is developing its own system for network management and control. As part of the development effort, American Express has determined what data it needs for effective network administration, and it now requires prospective suppliers of network management products to satisfy those data needs.

The shortcomings of network management tools are widely acknowledged, the subject of numerous articles in the field. Suppliers of those tools are struggling to meet the need and, in the process, capture a share of a rapidly growing market (variously estimated to be a few hundred million dollars in revenues per year). What users hope these products will provide are a simple, unified means for monitoring the performance of an entire network and alerting managers to failures or deterioration in performance; straightforward methods for analyzing and pinpointing the causes of problems; and a comprehensive set of tools for responding to problems and rerouting traffic around trouble spots. Management issues extend beyond the need to keep networks up and running, however. Also important, for example, are tools for controlling software distribution, preventing the introduction of unlicensed programs (which may contain viruses and other problems), and maintaining data integrity.

Ease of Use and Effective Presentation of Information

Simplicity, according to colloquium participants, is the ultimate determinant of an information network's effectiveness. If information technology is not easy to use, if information is not easy to access, select, and share, and if applications are not easily mastered, then an information and communication system fails to accomplish its primary function of enabling people.

For the average user, first impressions—that is, interactions with the user interface—can be lasting ones. Rather than breeding the familiarity that fosters greater use and exploration of network applications, several participants noted, differences in user interfaces can cause considerable frustration and confusion, dissuading employees, for example, from using electronic mail features or entering information into a database on potential customers. A networked information system, maintained Robert L. Martin, vice president for software technology and systems at Bell Communications Research, should have a "common look and feel." An underlying consistency in the appearance and functionality of applications and databases not only hastens learning and, perhaps, lowers expenditures for training employees who are expected to use the network, but it also makes it easier to tap the functionality of suites of applications.

With the emergence of multimedia applications that combine information in all its textual, graphical, and audio forms, new types of interfaces—those that, for example, respond to voice commands or eye and hand movements—will also be introduced. These offerings will greatly enhance the utility of information systems. But, said Larry E. Druffel, director of the Software Engineering Institute at Carnegie Mellon University, integrating new interface technology should not require revamping the information system and its underlying applications and databases.

Of course, the utility and diversity of applications and complementing tools determine what users can actually do with an information system. Today, most organizations have a backlog of ideas for new customized applications awaiting development. Ideally, workers or groups of workers should be able to build their own applications to help them accomplish their tasks. New organizational software that allows groups to work together is a step in this direction. It strives to create what, in essence, is a flexible programming environment that enables users to create their own applications. Such software often includes programming tools and prepackaged bits of programming code, or objects, that help users create new applications and databases by combining the components of existing ones. With significant advances over the next 10 to 15 years, suggested Weis of Sears, these programming aids may enable business professionals to "specify, in a nonprocedural way, the business functions that they want to perform and then turn those rules or nonprocedural statements into a system" that performs the desired applications. Today, however, the gap between promise and reality is large. Even for the most experienced systems integrators and software designers and programmers, it remains exceedingly difficult to develop an application or suite of applications that, at the implementation stage, works according to plans and expectations.

A major unsolved problem in this area is in the statement of requirements in a format understandable to the end users and also to the developers. These two groups usually come from very different job backgrounds and frequently share very little common terminology. Methods such as "rapid prototyping," which allow end users to observe the "look and feel" of the final systems before committing to full-scale development, have been very successful in defining expectations.

ISSUES AND RESEARCH NEEDS

Like the process of systems integration itself, the issues and challenges that will shape the evolution of distributed, networked computing must be assessed from several interrelated perspectives. A rapidly growing industry with a potentially large international market, the systems integration industry must attend to matters that will affect its competitive status. The businesses and other organizations that are now the primary users of systems integration services face challenges in making the most advantageous use of their information technology. Finally, as the web of interconnected computing and communication devices grows, the entire economy and all of U.S. society become affected, introducing a more encompassing set of needs and issues.

Today's experiences with networked information systems are testimony to the advantages to be reaped on scales small and large. But they are also testimony to the tremendous challenges positioned between the reality and the promise of information networking. One assessment of the current reality is this: "We have now reached a stage of uncontrolled chaos in the marketplace of data processing and data communications. Multivendor systems are almost universal, and the inability of the elements in this heterogeneous environment to interwork is legion."[11]

Many organizations have mastered these difficulties and are realizing significant benefits, but many are still struggling to take full advantage of their integrated systems of information technology. More important, most organizations, daunted, perhaps, by the prospect of sizable investments and the mire of technical issues, are not even pursuing many of the advantages afforded by information networking. At the colloquium, representatives of system integration firms and organizations that are major users of information technology offered their perspectives on the issues and research questions that stand in the way of effective use and wide-scale adoption of an information network by U.S. businesses. In subsequent chapters, many of these same issues are discussed in societal and global contexts.

Adapting the Installed Base of Information Technology

Information technology is a large and growing portion of the capital stock of U.S. businesses. A major challenge, therefore, is what many in the systems integration industry call migration, a "forward-engineering" process that enables owners of information technology to preserve and build on their installed bases of hardware, software, and information. Given the additional complexity this imposes on the already complex process of systems integration, it sometimes may seem that razing the existing system and starting anew is preferable to the often massive restructuring that moving to distributed, networked computing entails.

"Is our historical investment [in information technology] a plus or a minus?" asked Heller of Electronic Data Systems. The answer, according to other colloquium participants, is probably both, with the relative balance between asset or hindrance hinging on progress in developing methodologies for forward engineering and the reuse of software and databases (see section immediately below).

Unlike firms in Asia and, to a lesser but still significant degree, those in Europe, said Fischer of Andersen Consulting, U.S. organizations "have an enormous installed base of packaged knowledge, of business logic, of systems across the country. We cannot come in with a clean sheet of paper and say, 'Point B is where I want to be; A is where we are. Let's just do it.' We have got to have a way to recover design, to recover the logic out of the existing systems we have. . . . We need to be able to accumulate what has been done over the past 30 years with the automation projects, be able to collect that knowledge and that information in a repository, and be able to forward-engineer it to new solutions."

The issues involved transcend systems engineering, the act of connecting isolated devices and applications into networks. Improved systems engineering techniques are needed to strengthen the competitive status of the U.S. systems integration industry, according to Fischer and others. But far more challenging, they stressed, are the difficulties involved in restructuring existing technology and knowledge in ways so that this base both enhances and is enhanced by computing and communication capabilities.

Research on forward engineering and migration strategies is under way, much of it under the sponsorship of the U.S. Department of Defense. Thus far, however, the returns to these efforts have been limited. "Current reengineering technology," said Barry Boehm, director of the Defense Advanced Research Projects Agency (DARPA), "tends to take unstructured, outmoded ADP [automated data processing] systems and turn them into structured, outmoded ADP systems."

Software Design, Development, and Reuse

Every digital device is programmable. Software, therefore, is the glue that links the vast array of digital devices into a network, and through applications, it is the primary determinant of the network's value to an organization. It also represents the major expense of an integrated information system, much of it stemming from the customized programming involved and from the cost of maintaining and upgrading applications. In addition, poor software design and programming errors are not infrequent causes of network failures.

A recurring theme throughout the colloquium was the need to improve methods for software design and development to make the process more efficient and to make information systems more reliable. This is a long-recognized need, but, participants pointed out, its importance grows with the complexity of networked systems and with the size of the potential losses incurred when these systems fail.

Part of the answer rests with tools and techniques for reusing and inter-changing components of existing software, which are also essential for efforts to forward-engineer the installed base of information technology. "Often, the need to upgrade or change hardware, software, or communications [technology]," explained Heller of EDS, "requires companies to consider the necessity of reprogramming their existing applications to take advantage of the new advances in computer technology. To reduce this necessity, new tools—modeling, CASE [computer-aided software engineering], object-oriented techniques, and so on—need to be analyzed for their viability." Thus the ability to carry forward such things as the design rationale inherent in the software is an example of a subtle but important consideration in building large systems that must accommodate future developments.

"Today," Heller added, "application building is far too expensive."

Boehm of DARPA concurred: "[I]t is time to start building software component by component rather than construction by construction."

Methods for adapting and reusing existing programs in new applications and for restructuring old data are improving, some participants noted, citing progress in object-oriented programming as an example. Nonetheless, significant problems remain. Positive steps in this direction are continuing enhancement of CASE tools for computer-aided program development, object-oriented techniques for using preprogrammed bits of software, formal techniques for verifying whether programming code performs according to specifications, and nonprocedural languages that permit users to write their own programs without using a formal programming language. For now, it is uncertain whether one method or a combination of these methods will yield improvements on the scale that is needed.

Several panelists suggested that object-oriented techniques hold considerable promise in achieving interoperability among the functions within separate applications and in salvaging past programming work. CASE tools, in contrast, they observed, have yet to yield the promised productivity benefits. Indeed, in a recent survey of users of CASE tools, more than a third reported that programming productivity had not increased.[12]

In the meantime Japanese software firms and, recently, European companies are concentrating on manufacturing-style approaches to software development. Approaches vary, but quality-assurance methods and automation are common denominators.

Methodologies to Guide Organizational Change

Full assimilation of an integrated information system often implies a corresponding integration of the business organization and its processes. Typically, this may entail flattening the organizational hierarchy, revamping the scope of business, and linking units that were once functionally isolated. Such sweeping change is not accomplished easily. But experiences of the last two decades demonstrate that the competitive advantages gained by automating the status quo evaporate quickly.

Many systems integration firms use formal methods for analyzing how firms use and communicate information internally and externally. On the basis of such analyses and close consultation with their clients, integrators develop an architectural plan for "defining technology requirements," said Heller of EDS, and for "blending . . . investments in computing and communication [equipment and software] and in structuring data into information that is meaningful in business terms." Nonetheless, he added, the process is a "little bit fuzzy."

"There are a lot of disciplines required," he said. "Not all of these disciplines are strictly technical or technology-based. But it takes a multidisciplinary team approach, in our experience, to deliver to a customer, to meet his requirements in even small areas that are well bounded, to say nothing of a full business."

Because each organization is unique, it would be unreasonable to assume that systems integration and the implementation of changes in business operations and worker relationships can be reduced entirely to a formal methodology. Still, better tools are needed, according to Fischer of Andersen Consulting. "We need some packaged or agreed-to methods and tools to help us figure out how to go about redesigning the business process," he said.

It can be helpful to view the systems integration process in a total life-cycle perspective, one that includes "change" as a built-in attribute. One model suggested had five steps: first, identifying the need for change from the current operation; second, defining and documenting the requirements for the "new" system; third, implementing and integrating the components of the new system; fourth, making the transition from the current system to the new system with acceptable risk to the business; and fifth, maintaining the new system, including providing for quality improvements and upgrades (which takes us back to the first step).

Standardization

When the topic of standards arises in a group of hardware manufacturers and software publishers, a heated debate can be expected to ensue. In general terms, one group will argue that standards can prematurely freeze technology and dampen innovation, while the other group extols the merits of easy connectivity and interoperability for users and, consequently, the market-enlarging effects of standards. No such debate occurred at the colloquium. Suppliers of systems integration services and users of information technology appeared united in their support for standardization of hardware and software interfaces and for communication protocols.

"Standardization does not imply a static situation," said Heller of EDS. "Standards must be continually reviewed and modified as requirements change and technology advances."

Added Crawford of American Express, "International standardization and so-called open systems will add further impetus to systems integration."

While espousing the need for standardization, several speakers were critical of how U.S. industry, the federal government, and users of information technology have participated in the standards-setting process. U.S. computer and communications firms are active in national and international standards organizations, but too rarely do they act from an industrywide perspective. Although increasing numbers of users are becoming more active in standards issues, sometimes crafting their own standards, most remain passive observers.

Crawford advised users to "be proactive" in standards issues. Two staff members in his division work full-time to advance American Express's positions on international telecommunications standards, and another small group of workers concentrate on regulatory and standards activities in the United States.

Several colloquium participants suggested that the federal government could play an instrumental role in coordinating U.S. industry's participation in international standards activities and monitoring developments in foreign countries. They pointed out that Japan and the European Community have taken a more comprehensive and forward-looking view of standards than have U.S. government and industry.

Careful monitoring of international activities, said Hopper of American Airlines, is necessary because of the impact of standards on the globalization of information technology and because of the potential for nations to devise standards that serve to protect domestic industries and restrict international competition. "I am a believer that standards can only help us," he said. "We should embrace them and not resist their inevitability, but with the caveat that we have to guard against standards" that are designed to be barriers to international competition.

Other facets of standardization are discussed in following chapters (see Chapter 3 appendix on standards making).

Data Communication Capabilities

As already noted, large U.S. businesses have invested enormous sums to build their own high-speed communication links to connect networks. Many have chosen to bypass, as much as they can, the public telecommunications carriers because of insufficient data-carrying capacity,[13] discontinuities in the service offerings of local and regional carriers, and cost savings they can achieve with their own networks. These firms have, in effect, built their own information infrastructure, an unaffordable option for most organizations that could benefit from high-speed internetworking capabilities. Thus most of the approximately 700,000 private networks in the United States are information outposts linked by the data-transmission equivalent of one-lane highways.[14]

As discussed in the next chapter, the prospect of broadband Integrated Services Digital Network service, which initially would offer transmission rates of more than 150 million bits per second, is viewed as one potential remedy to this infrastructural deficiency.

Personnel Needs

Many colloquium participants suggested that the growth of the U.S. systems integration industry could be constrained by shortages of qualified personnel. While the entire computer sector confronts scarcities of talent in key science and engineering disciplines, the needs of systems integrators may be the most difficult to satisfy, at least through the traditional channel of universities.

"Systems integration demands a special mix of expertise with emphasis on organizational, consulting, and management skills—on top of demonstrated technical expertise," Crawford explained. "There is no way that recent graduates can acquire those skills through education alone."

Nonetheless, participants maintained that U.S. universities have an important education and training role to play. Unfortunately, departments of computer science and engineering and other units that concentrate on computer-related topics have not included systems integration in their domains. "The best way to get the academic community to address the introduction of systems integration into the educational system is to entice the academics to engage in appropriate research," said Druffel of the Software Engineering Institute at Carnegie Mellon University. "We must develop within the research community an appreciation for the importance of the problem and its validity as a research topic. This also implies the availability of funding, and so the major research funding agencies must be convinced [of the need]."

Currently, many systems integration firms invest heavily in the training of their employees. EDS and Andersen Consulting, for example, spend the equivalent of about 10 percent of their annual revenues on training programs. The need for these programs will likely remain strong, according to Heller.

"Retraining will be one of the key strategies of systems integration firms for meeting their technical personnel needs," Heller said. However, the challenge of equipping people with the requisite skills and knowledge may become more difficult, he said. "Technical positions in a systems integration firm require technical aptitude, and many people undergoing training will not be successful," he explained. At the same time, the field is becoming more complex. "The technical curricula a company uses for training entry-level science and engineering graduates will likely require modification in pace and content," Heller said. Moreover, imparting technical skills to people with nontechnical backgrounds "will require much patience and leadership attention."

NOTES

1. For a broad range of historical statistical information see *The Computer, Business Equipment, Software and Services, and Telecommunications Industry: 1960-1996*, Industry Marketing Statistics Committee, CBEMA, Washington, D.C., 1987.

2. Gantz, John. 1987. "Systems Integration: Living in a House of Our Own Making," *Telecommunication Products + Technology*, May, p. 35. Gantz, John. 1991. "Double Trouble," *The Economist*, January 12, p. 63. Depke, Deirdre A., and Richard Brandt. 1991. "PCs: What the Future Holds," *Business Week*, August 12, pp. 58-64.

3. Wright, Karen. 1990. "The Road to the Global Village," *Scientific American*, March, p. 84.

4. General Accounting Office. 1990. *Meeting the Government's Technology Challenge*, GAO/IMTEC-90-23, February, p. 4.

5. Verity, John W. 1990. "Taming the Wild Network," *Business Week*, Oct. 8, p. 144. Dauber, Steven M. 1991. "Finding Fault," *Byte*, March, p. 207.

6. For example, in July of 1991 what eventually turned out to be a "minor" software problem led to massive failures of telephone networks in several large metropolitan areas, including Washington, D.C., and Los Angeles (Andrews, Edmund L. 1991. "String of Phone Failures Perplexes Companies and U.S. Investigators," *New York Times*, July 3, p. A1).

7. Computer Science and Telecommunications Board, National Research Council. 1991. *Computers at Risk: Safe Computing in the Information Age*, National Academy Press, Washington, D.C., p. 7.

8. For example, the major airline reservation networks and service providers are now going through an expensive process of replacing their widely used but proprietary airline protocol, the Airline Link Control (ALC) with its 6-bit-per-character structure, in favor of standard packet-switching communication technology widely available on the open market (see Crockett, Barton. 1990. "Airline Reservation Nets Finally See Fit to Dump Outdated Protocols," *Network World*, September 24, p. 9).

9. In fact, GM defined a new standard (Manufacturing Automation Protocol, or MAP) for the specific needs of this application. MAP is now used widely in plant-

floor automation systems. See Kaminski, Michael A. 1990. "The Users' Viewpoint on Standards-Based Communications," *Crossroads of Information Technology Standards*, National Academy Press, Washington, D.C., p. 11.

10. Dorros, Irwin. 1990. "Calling for Cooperation," *Bellcore Exchange*, November-December, p. 7.

11. Kleinrock, Leonard. 1991. "ISDN—The Path to Broadband Networks," *Proceedings of the IEEE*, Vol. 79, No. 2, February, p. 112.

12. Brandt, Richard. 1991. "Can the U.S. Stay Ahead in Software?" *Business Week*, March 11, p. 104.

13. Public telephone companies now offer two types of enhanced service for transmission of digital data. T1 service transmits data at the rate of 1.5 million bits per second, sufficient for simultaneous transmission of voice communication and textual and numerical data; T3 service offers a transmission rate of about 45 million bits per second, which accommodates only rudimentary real-time graphics applications.

14. Gilder, George. 1991. "Into the Telecosm," *Harvard Business Review*, March-April, pp. 150-161.

3

Enabling Technology:
Communications and Software

Before our very eyes the now ubiquitous computer is undergoing a profound metamorphosis from a largely stand-alone, all-in-one machine to a gateway to a world of information technology and services. Indeed, for many people today, the computer is as much a communications device as it is a machine that performs high-speed mathematical and logical calculations. Not coincidentally, with each new wave of technology, the now ubiquitous digital telephone becomes ever more like the computer. As this convergence of computing and communications technology proceeds, it is not entirely clear whether the distinction between the two will have any meaning.

Driving this convergence is the as of yet unabating miniaturization of electronic components that make up integrated circuits. As the density of the components on integrated circuits has increased at exponential rates, the speed and power of computers and other digital equipment have improved tremendously, while their costs have moved steadily downward. For example, workstations have been almost exclusively the tools of scientists and engineers. Fast and able to run several applications simultaneously, the high-performance machines have been too expensive for the average personal computer user. But workstation prices are dropping rapidly, and, by the end of the decade, some people predict, the equivalents of today's high-end machines may sell for well below $1,000, making the technology affordable for large numbers of people. Already, a well-equipped personal computer based on an Intel 80386 processor running UNIX can be purchased for about $3,000, or about the cost (in current dollars) of the much more primitive IBM PCs in the early 1980s.

The predictable and high rate of progress in hardware has fueled rising expectations for distributed information networks of immense capacity, capability, flexibility, and reach. These expectations, however, are constrained by technical, regulatory, and economic challenges on national and international levels. The principal obstacles lie in the areas of telecommunications and software technology, commonly referred to as the "bottlenecks" that impede progress toward large-scale information networks offering widely available services. Simply stated, the technical problems are these: First, the information processing capabilities of computers greatly exceed the capabilities of public telecommunication carriers to transmit data in its many forms between remote computers; data arrive in trickles rather than in the torrents that are needed to support real-time, multimedia interactive computing. Second, advances in hardware have outraced the ability of software designers and computer programmers to develop applications that exploit the full capabilities of new devices. The gap between potential performance and the actual functionality supplied by software applications remains large, and, at the same time, software accounts for a large and growing expense in the development of information technology. Third is a combined telecommunications and software problem. Software of high reliability and quality is a critical component of efforts to improve the transmission capacity and capabilities of telecommunications carriers, as evidenced by the fact that software may account for as much as 80 percent of the cost of a telecommunications system.[1,2] Building an infrastructure and implementing the associated services necessary to achieve the seamless connection of information networks on national and global scales pose large, complex challenges for software development. Finally, it is not enough to develop technological solutions to the impediments that prevent high-speed, high-performance networking. There must also be agreement between the telecommunications and computer industries on how those solutions should be implemented into standards. Moreover, to promote global networking, standards development within nations should complement the work of international standards-setting bodies.

Although telecommunications and software issues loom large, technical challenges also face manufacturers of integrated circuits and the other hardware components of information technology. For example, in addition to new software, faster and more powerful microprocessors, perhaps using photonic technology, will be needed to achieve the high switching speeds necessary for rapid transmission between computers of large volumes of data in multimedia forms. Moreover, as communications performance improves, computers and other digital equipment, whose capabilities are now constrained by slow data transmission, will eventually be hard pressed to assimilate data arriving at rates exceeding a billion bits per second, as envisioned for the National Research and Education Network (NREN), a component of the recently begun federal High Performance Computing and Communications (HPCC) program.

"Multi-gigabit networks represent a change in kind, not just degree, from today's networks," a committee of the Federal Coordinating Council for Science, Engineering, and Technology has explained. "For example, consider that in a coast-to-coast communication at three gigabits [3 billion bits] per second there are at any instant 'in flight' nearly nine megabytes [million bytes, or groups of eight bits] of data, which is more than the memory of most personal computers and workstations."[3]

At the colloquium, most of the discussion focused on issues related to software and communications. Participants also addressed some of the challenges confronting the HPCC program and, in particular, the NREN.

COMMUNICATIONS SURVEY

A rule of thumb, based on today's networking experiences with traditional technology, is that the speed and ease of communication decrease as a function of distance. The fastest data flows occur within a computer, via the data bus, or the set of wires that shuttle signals between the microprocessor and circuit boards containing memory and controlling input and output devices. In local area networks (LANs) linked by coaxial cable, the typical rate for transmitting data between computers is 10 million bits per second. Data communication between LANs linked by a wide area network slows to a figurative snail's pace. The maximum data-carrying capacity of a typical copper wire telephone line is 64,000 bits per second, but modems generally do not even make full use of this limited capacity, with most transmitting and receiving data at rates between 2,400 and 19,200 bits per second. Specialized data transmission services—called T1 and T3—offered by telephone companies can greatly improve this rate, to 1.5 million bits per second for T1 and 45 million bits per second for T3.

But even at a rate of 45 million bits per second, correspondence between remote computers is too slow to support interactive, data-intensive tasks, especially sophisticated graphics applications. Consider, for example, that one still image contains between 20 million and 200 million bits of information; in digital form, a typical pair of chest X-rays contains the information equivalent of four volumes (text) of the *Encyclopedia Britannica*.[4] Also consider the data-carrying capacities necessary for the following uses of information technology: real-time graphics applications run on remote supercomputers require rates of 50 million to more than 700 million bits per second per user; real-time, cooperative computer-aided-design systems require 1.5 million bits per user; and television-quality video and audio require 45 million bits per channel, or less than half the rate for digital high-definition television (without data compression techniques).[5-7]

Introducing the need to integrate textual, graphical, and audio information for multimedia presentations magnifies the need for high-speed transmission, as does increasing the number of users on the network.

Fiber-optic technology figures prominently in proposed measures to enhance transmission capacities and to integrate multimedia forms of data. Indeed, the fiber-optical lines that handle about 95 percent of long-distance telephone calls in the United States transmit information at a rate of about 2 billion bits per second. With the information-carrying capacity, or bandwidth, of fiber-optic cable increasing a hundredfold over the past decade, bandwidths of a trillion bits per second may be not only achievable but also commercially practical in the next decade.

Moreover, the declining cost of optical fiber has made it competitive with copper wire for even short-distance communication links. In terms of maintenance and upkeep, fiber offers economic advantages over copper wire. Some local telephone companies are running fiber from their central switching offices to remote distribution terminals that handle up to 1,000 lines and, from there, to streetside pedestals that link to individual homes and most businesses. The cost of completing the final stretch, from curbside to home, remains prohibitive.[8] Thus it is not clear when fiber will be extended to residences and businesses; nor is it certain whether local telephone companies will be the primary actors. Cable television companies, which have strung coaxial cable to 60 percent of U.S. homes and could easily connect nearly 30 percent more,[9] appear eager to exploit fiber-optic technology, and some have announced their intentions to run fiber to the home.[10] Incentives for completing this important last step, whether done by telephone companies, cable companies, or others, are dependent not only on perceptions of the market for services made possible by fiber-optic connections, but also on regulations governing the behavior of segments of the communication industry. (Regulatory issues are discussed in the next chapter.)

Integrated Services Digital Network Service

What is clear, however, is that many of the basic tools exist for sending and receiving multimedia information. Moreover, a world vision of high-speed communication networks already exists in the form of integrated services digital network (ISDN) service.[11] A slowly evolving concept consuming the attention of industry, national, and international standards-making bodies since the mid-1970s, ISDN is essentially a telecommunications view of a public information infrastructure. It will allow users and carriers to aggregate, or multiplex, transmissions of data in graphical, textual, and audio forms, permitting multimedia communication between users on a network.

In its first and current manifestation, however, ISDN offers data transmission at a rate far less than 1 percent of the 150 million bits per second needed for real-time interactive multimedia applications. So-called narrowband ISDN (NISDN) service can carry 144,000 bits per second via two 64,000-bit-per-second channels and one 16,000-bit-per-second channel. Communications are delivered through a standard telephone socket and are parceled out to telephone and computer, which are linked by wire. With this setup, remote computer users can converse by telephone and simultaneously exchange alphanumeric information, which appears on the screens of their terminals. In the United States, about 0.5 percent of equipped access lines supported NISDN as of 1990; many of these were installed to serve the private networks of large companies, partially reducing their need for separate transmission lines for voice and data communications.[12]

Although the simultaneous linkage of telephone and computer afforded by the initial ISDN offering is significant, data transmission speeds do not accommodate many types of applications of information technology, and they are greatly exceeded by service offerings already available, such as T3. Moreover, users of ISDN service may have to invest in new equipment interfaces. (For example, an ISDN adapter for a personal computer, with accompanying software, costs about $2,200). In essence, early offerings of ISDN service enhance the capabilities of the telephone but leave untapped the potential of the computer as a tool for sharing, processing, and presenting information in multimedia forms.

Successive upgrades in ISDN service are in the offing, however. From 144,000 bits per second, rates would improve first to 1.54 million bits (24 channels, each carrying 64,000 bits per second), a service already used by some businesses. From there, rates would move progressively higher, to the 150-million-bit-per-second threshold for multimedia applications and upward to gigabit-per-second speeds.

The migration to the threshold rate (i.e., 150 million bits per second), which marks the transition to broadband ISDN (BISDN), has been frustratingly slow for users awaiting high-speed distributed computing networks that are interoperable, accommodate a broad range of interactive applications, and are easy to negotiate. These users want BISDN to be available now rather than at the turn of the century or beyond. As a result, many are forging their own solutions to their needs for high-speed communication and incurring the expense of building private networks.

One argument for proceeding with NISDN contends that the initial service is a necessary stepping-stone to broadband public networks. For example, while large corporations appear to have an insatiable appetite for communications bandwidth, many smaller businesses and most households may see little need for digital information services, much less a single access point to those services, which ISDN would provide. If a reasonable level of demand is established for NISDN applications, then telecommunications carriers and manufacturers of telecommunications equipment would be encouraged to invest in the technologies required to progress to BISDN.

Perhaps an even more compelling argument is the growing status of ISDN as an international standard interface for global networking. Government-owned communications monopolies in Japan and Europe seem to be more convinced of this argument than are U.S. telecommunications carriers and information-service providers. As a result, implementation of supporting ISDN standards has been proceeding more rapidly in Japan, Singapore, and Europe than in the United States. However, in early 1991, major U.S. computer and communications firms endorsed a set of standard specifications for ISDN service.[13] The agreement could lead to conversion of about half of subscriber lines to NISDN service by the end of 1994.[14]

Toward Broadband Networks

ISDN's modest beginnings might be likened to a narrow river that over time broadens into a major waterway supporting cargo-carrying vessels of every size and function and, by means of its tributaries, offering access to any port desired. Rather than on geological time scales, however, the transformation from today's constricted narrowband communication networks into broadband arteries with immense data-carrying capacity is expected take place over the span of a few decades.

Fiber-optic technology offers the means for achieving this transformation, but the evolution requires more than glass cables serving as conduits for multigigabit streams of data. In its early stages, the evolution may largely entail pushing the limits of current technology, but moving to gigabit-per-second rates and beyond will require revolutionary changes in computing and communication networks. "As we move into gigabit networks, however, we must take a 'clean sheet' approach to many of the systems issues," writes Leonard Kleinrock, professor of computer science at the University of California, Los Angeles. "The critical areas to be considered include switching technology, processor interfaces, protocols, connection-oriented communications, routing, layered architectures, and coexistence with carrier environments."[15]

Whither OSI?

Some of the challenges that Kleinrock has identified could require a major revamping of the International Standards Organization's Open Systems Interconnection (OSI) architecture. Essentially a composite reference model for building information systems, OSI was devised to promote the development of industrywide standard protocols to create a common communications environment for distributed systems.[16] (See Box 3.1, "A Simple

Box 3.1 A Simple Protocol Analog

"The diplomatic use of the term 'protocol,' as a code of etiquette and precedence derived from the Greek roots 'to glue together,' comes close to its meaning in computer networks. The messages that flow between computers follow an established set of rules (etiquette) in proper sequence to glue the network into a cooperating community. The following human analog tries to capture the concept of a protocol hierarchy or stack.

"An American chief executive officer (CEO) wishes to complete a business transaction with his or her counterpart (peer) in Japan. The American CEO, representing the 'application layer,' composes thoughts in a manner that a Japanese peer will understand (peer protocol), and dictates a letter to a secretary (presentation layer). The secretary converts the communication from one format (voice) to another format (written), representing the service the secretary (lower layer) provides to the boss (higher layer). The secretary then puts the letter in an envelope and puts the Japanese CEO's address on the envelope, thus making a session on behalf of a higher-layer entity. The letter is mailed (passed down to a lower-layer entity) to the U.S. Postal Service, a reliable 'datagram' transport mechanism. The post office passes the letter to regional collection centers (switching centers of the network layer) and then on to the destination post office via the routing information in the letter's address, usually the ZIP code (control information). The passing is handled by bundling many different letters with similar ZIP codes in bags carried by truck, plane, or ship to the destination (the physical media, lowest layer). The process now repeats in reverse— post office to secretary to Japanese CEO—physical to network to transport to presentation to application layer. The Japanese secretary sees to it that the English letter is translated into Japanese, the destination's presentation layer.

"At each layer of the protocol hierarchy, there is a peer protocol that understands the rules (etiquette) of its peers; the letters are formatted the same, the envelopes are addressed the same, the mailbags are labeled in an agreed-upon format, and so on throughout the process. Furthermore, each layer provides a service to its higher layer, and interface protocols express the service requests. Figure [3.1] shows this hierarchy of layers: the popular Open System Interconnect (OSI) model of a seven-layer hierarchy."

SOURCE: Computer Science and Technology Board, National Research Council. 1988. *Global Trends in Computer Technology and Their Impact on Export Control*, National Academy Press, Washington, D.C., pp. 110-11.

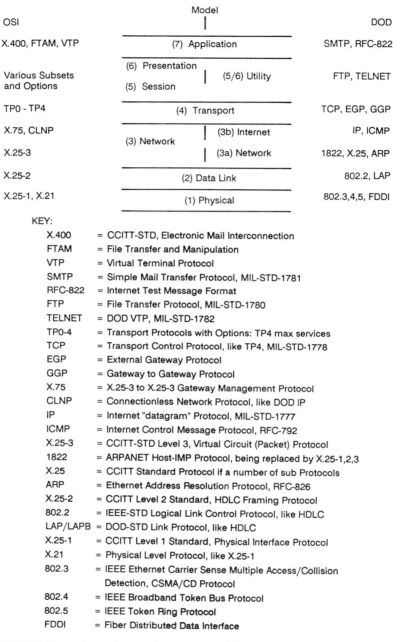

FIGURE 3.1   Open System Interconnect (OSI) and DOD models with representative protocols. SOURCE: Computer Science and Technology Board, National Research Council. 1988. *Global Trends in Computer Technology and Their Impact on Export Control*, National Academy Press, Washington, D.C., p. 112.

Protocol Analog.") OSI divides the workings of a network into seven layers, each composed of one or more protocols. The bottom two layers—"physical" and "data link"—specify transmission rates, signaling conventions, and other protocols for managing communications media. At the top, or "applications" layer, are the protocols for electronic mail and other applications that can be conducted on the network. OSI embodied more than 100 international standards as of 1989,[17] and the number continues to grow. Most of the protocols, however, attend to the transfer of data; very few pertain to high-level collaborative applications that can be performed over a network.

Robert Martin of Bellcore was one of several colloquium participants who suggested that rather than fostering information networking, standards are becoming so unwieldy that they may eventually deter its evolution. "The thing I worry most about is the number and the inherent complexity," he said. "We are not smart enough to manage within this environment."

Alfred Aho, also of Bellcore, had a similar lament. "By the time you look at the total amount of software required to develop the system according to the OSI world," he said, "you are talking about millions of lines of code. If we move forward into the future, we are going to have components of the systems we are building today for years into the future. Who is going to maintain that old software? Who is going to understand it? What kind of return on investment are we going to get for people who look after this old software and make fixes to it when the systems malfunction?"

One of the penalties paid for the "openness" that OSI is intended to foster may be exacted in the form of reduced speed, a problem explained by Hisashi Kobayashi, dean of engineering and applied science at Princeton University. Gigabit transmission rates could overwhelm current and emerging communication protocols designed to support the OSI reference model, which has guided standards development for more than a decade. "It is still too early to say," he explained, "but people are beginning to realize that the OSI layered architecture will be inefficient for a network based on optical technology. Communication links will no longer be a bottleneck, but most likely processing power [of switches] will be." Processing power at network switches could be especially taxed when data flows approach gigabit-per-second speeds.

In a typical packet-switched network, the switch must process three layers of OSI protocols before sending data en route on to its intended destination. The intelligence required to process these "heavyweight" protocols causes switching delays of 50 to 100 milliseconds, which are tolerable when data is traveling at a rate of 64 thousand bits per second. As rates improve to hundreds of millions of bits and higher, the delays could create the equivalent of rush-hour traffic jams. In Kobayashi's view, protocols for broadband networks will have to be simpler to enable fast response times and to avoid overtaxing the processing capabilities of switches, as well as of computers communicating on the network. "Lightweight" protocols, which may trade some of the functionality of OSI standards for greater speed, should be a focus of research, he suggested, adding that some of the tasks now performed by software may be more efficiently carried out by hardware.

In fact, switching hardware itself may have to change. Processing and transmission demands may eventually exceed the speed and capabilities of silicon-based integrated circuit electronic devices. Faster gallium-arsenide semiconductors would yield substantial improvements in switching performance, but in the long term, photoelectronic, photonic, and perhaps even superconducting devices may be the sources of the revolutionary advances in switching technology that many think will be needed to meet future networking demands.[18]

Moreover, current protocols assume that errors and data losses are most likely to originate in the network, and procedures have been devised to guard against such problems. But with a high-speed optical-fiber network, Kobayashi explained, "the traditional notion of error due to noise in the channel is less relevant than the possible loss of packaged information due to the finite memory space in the buffer," where data awaiting transmission is temporarily stored.

Also problematic, he said, are network control and management. Today, feedback mechanisms are used to ease network congestion: A message is sent to the sending terminal, which then slows its transmission or waits until the bottleneck is cleared. But with gigabit transmission rates, streams of data packets already will be in transit by the time the network can alert the sending terminal to its traffic problems. This means that, instead of reactive or feedback control, methods of "predictive or proactive control" are likely to be needed. "In other words, you have to predict the congestion a few milliseconds or nanoseconds ahead of time and then take some corrective action to limit the transmission of your information," Kobayashi explained.

Integrating Communications Media

In recent years, wireless communication services have proliferated, placing heavy demands on the already crowded frequency bands of the radio spectrum used for, among other things, radio, television, satellite-to-ground telephone services, cellular and mobile telephones, and pagers. Pending uses for the over-the-air communication channels include computer-to-computer radio connections and personal communications networks. With some exceptions, these services stand apart from those offered over copper wire and fiber-optic cable—public telephone service and data communications. For example, the fast-growing cellular telephone industry, which has seen its subscribership increase dramatically to 5.3 million in 1990[19] and the public switched network are evolving as separate islands rather than as complementary components within a larger communications environment.

Observers have called for a reexamination of communication options, with the ultimate aim of integrating now-fragmented wireless and wire-line services into a coherent framework for internetworking. Some would go even further. For example, there have been suggestions for transmitting television signals by means of fiber-optic cable, rather than over the air. This possibility is created by proposals for an all-digital high-definition television (HDTV) standard for the United States. (The U.S. Federal Communications Commission is evaluating six proposals for an HDTV transmission standard, four of which are all-digital systems. The commission is expected to make its selection in 1993.) The large segment of the spectrum now consumed by private and public television stations would be freed for other uses, and at the same time, the new means of delivering video entertainment might create levels of consumer demand sufficient to justify extending fiber-optic cable to U.S. households, completing all the connections necessary for a nationwide broadband communications infrastructure.

SOFTWARE

Part and parcel of many issues and obstacles confronting telecommunications carriers and service providers are those related to the design, development, and maintenance of software. As Aho of Bellcore suggested with his predictions of problems associated with OSI protocols, complex standards are underlain by complex software. Even in a single self-contained network, general management and housekeeping tasks, such as routing, addressing, error checking, and protocol implementation, may account for more than 90 percent of the data traffic.[20]

The concerns raised by Aho are part of a set of issues collectively referred to as the "software problem." The manifestations of the problem are several. Advances in hardware have outraced the ability of software designers and computer programmers to develop applications that exploit the capabilities of new devices. New applications are often beset with errors, and, in the opinion of many observers, they are difficult to use. Modifying old programs and databases to work with new hardware or new software is time consuming and expensive, exacerbating a backlog in new applications awaiting development. Applications developed to work with one operating system do not easily transfer to another. Consequently, one frequently cited testimonial to technological progress—that today's personal computers are equivalent to the mainframes of less than a decade ago—is diminished by the fact that available software takes far less than full advantage of the raw processing power of the modestly priced machines now sitting on millions of desks.

The trend toward open systems, improvements in tools to aid designers and programmers, and other developments have paid dividends. Nonetheless, software design and development have proven especially resistant to efforts to transform these activities into a structured engineering discipline, a transformation that, many believe, would contribute directly to progress in distributed network computing. To many, the process is a curious combination of art and craft, particularly during the early stages of conceptualization and design, and of laborious writing of programming code.[21]

"Software may be the limiting factor," said Larry Druffel of Carnegie Mellon University's Software Engineering Institute. "But remember the other side of that: it is the enabling factor as well. . . . Obviously, if we are going to do systems integration [on a national scale], we really have to deal with the software issues because that is, after all, what allows us to change things after they are built. That is what it is all about."

Colloquium participants examined some of the hurdles that must be overcome to improve software design and development and to manage the increasing complexity inherent in integrating information systems.

Measures of Complexity and Performance

Even in small-scale projects, according to Aho, systems integration poses the challenge of transforming abstractions, such as improved customer service or product quality, into concrete functions, usually embodied in software applications. Consider one of today's popular user interfaces, a graphical model of the desktop: It is an abstraction that transforms a computer screen into the most common of work environments.

In the process of creating systems of systems, each successive layer of integration introduces new abstractions underlain by higher levels of complexity, Aho explained. It becomes increasingly difficult, he added, to assess the performance and effectiveness of systems. Consequently, integration strategies that work well in the context of a single system may be undermined by unanticipated interactions and problems that arise as the scale of internetworking grows.

"I am a great fan of looking at problems in a systems context," Aho said. "So, the one thing I would advocate to my fellow researchers is that when you do your work, do the work in a systems context. Ask, does this scale up to medium-sized systems and to large-sized systems? We are making substantial investments in [integrating systems], and we would like to be able to design systems that are not the [equivalents] of Three Mile Island."

The design of integrated systems, he suggested, would benefit greatly from measures that could help integrators and researchers define the complexity and scale of their undertakings. Similarly, Aho advocated developing measures for gauging the performance of systems, such as their cost-effectiveness, how easily they can incorporate new technology and accommodate new applications, and how they respond to accidents and failures. Implicit in Aho's remarks is the importance of an interdisciplinary perspective.

"My theory is that, if you do not look at the sum of the performance measures and the underlying architecture, then there will be untoward events in the future, which will cause the systems to behave adversely [and very badly]," Aho explained. "We would like to have some kind of performance guarantees in the running of systems that they will respond gracefully to adverse inputs. We have lots of examples of systems that have behaved badly under certain conditions."

One method being used with increasing effectiveness in the marketplace to measure the quality of systems integration, software, and hardware is the use of Service-Level Agreements (SLAs) as a contract between the providers of services and the users. The SLA specifically lists measurable attributes such as "up-time," response time for user transactions, cost per user hour, and other quantitative items that can be used by both the provider and the consumer to evaluate the quality of service. Definition of an SLA also helps in setting expectations for the system at the beginning of the development and integration process.

Software Architecture

The traditional definition of architecture—the art and science of designing and erecting buildings—continues to dominate thinking in systems integration, according to Druffel of Carnegie Mellon University. That is, systems designers tend to think in terms of configurations of hardware, just as building architects translate their concepts into specifications for components made of iron and steel.

"That is kind of what we have been dealing with over the years," Druffel said. "First, we have a hardware architecture and then the software guys have to figure out some way to make all that work. As we think about systems architectural issues, we really need to think about the complementary software architectures. From a software perspective, I would like to know, for example, the functional view, the control structures, the expected behavior, how [system] states are stored and communicated, and what the dependencies are."

Druffel and others underscored the need for standards (see below, "Software Standards") and other mechanisms that foster a shared perspective on software architecture and better communication among dispersed groups involved in developing systems software. At their current stage of development, object-oriented programming techniques, CASE tools, and "layered abstractions," such as the OSI model, represent only a partial response to the need, Druffel said, and, in some cases, they interject additional confusion. "Each of these approaches reflects a different notion about what services it provides," he explained. "If you are going to write software that tries to interconnect them, it gets rather messy."

"A good example of the problems you run into when people are building tools or building components that are later going to be integrated," he added, "are those that arise from different views of data ownership." Often, it is not clear which group within a distributed computing environment has responsibility for database control and management, or several groups may assume authority. In either case, Druffel said, configuration management—essentially, organizing the construction of complex software from separate pieces—and control of software versions can be problematic. Moreover, system components may be designed by people who differ in their views of data ownership, resulting in different models of how the overall system and its pieces should function. When the time comes to integrate these differently conceived components, difficulties often arise.

The need for a shared architectural view is magnified by the goal of developing systems that can evolve with technology, a recurring colloquium theme. However, this goal can confound software development. "When we are talking about software," Druffel said, "we are talking about components that are going to be developed probably without complete knowledge of how they are going to be used, and we are talking about systems that have to evolve. That is, they are going to be composed of units without a complete understanding of what that end system may eventually be, which adds a little bit of complication to the issue."

The added criterion of evolvability presents software developers with the task of planning for all technological possibilities. At best, developers can only approximate future developments. So rather than being a rigid scaffolding that greatly restricts future options for expansion, software architecture must have a high degree of flexibility. Adoption of new technology and new applications should not require razing the previous system and starting anew.

"We know that over the next 10 years," Aho said, "progress in microelectronics is going to make computer chips faster, memories bigger, and bandwidths greater, and we should not forget about algorithms and other procedures that will be making our software faster. Are systems designers going to be able to accommodate these improvements?"

Aho suggested that Japanese methods of incremental quality improvement may be applicable to systems design. "Proof of progress over time," he said, should be a hallmark, but operationalizing a model of quality improvement poses a "very difficult challenge for the systems design community."

Software Standards

Standards are an essential element of a coherent software architecture. Unfortunately, promulgation of common conventions and widely accepted platforms for linking applications and other software elements is as prone to delays and other complications as is standards making in the telecommunications area. In fact, development of software-related standards to achieve true interoperability of applications may be a more formidable task, beset by more interdependencies and greater levels of detail. To convey this complexity, Druffel provided a small list of topics awaiting internetworking standards: data bindings, language bindings, and bindings between standards, network management, and security. Performing an application on a distributed computing network may invoke standards in all these areas, as well as additional ones.

Moreover, each area presents its own peculiar set of issues. For example, a standard that is intended to bridge the incompatibilities between different programming languages must not only serve as a translator but also resolve other disparities. "It is not just a matter of syntactically communicating between two languages," Druffel explained. "They really do have different run-time expectations. Under one language, a default may mean something entirely different from what it means in the other language. These kinds of issues have to be dealt with as well."

Consider also all the eventualities and interdependencies that must be addressed to enable group collaboration on multimedia documents that combine, for example, voice input, graphics, digitized photographs, handwritten notes, spreadsheet tabulations, and keyboard input. The capability to exchange heterogeneous types of information between points anywhere along a network and to combine the elements of this diverse compilation according to the whims of users will require an array of standards and common conventions. But if these standards require users to perform laborious routines and entail time-consuming steps, the benefits of collaboration will be diluted.

Converging Software Interests

Since networking, in general, and interoperability, in particular, are the major motivations for standards making in these and many other technical areas, distinctions between what is a computing standard and what is a communication standard have become almost artificial. However, the landscape of national and international standards making is divided between the two realms and then subdivided among industry domains within each. (See appendix below for a brief description of major standards-making bodies.) Although some consolidation of activities and interests has occurred in recent years, it has not matched rates of consolidation occurring between the communications and computer industries and between the information services and applications supported by those industries.

"Over the last 20 years," Kleinrock of UCLA has maintained, "the innovations in data networking have come from the data-processing industry, and not from the carriers. This is in spite of the fact that the data-processing solutions have used the underlying carrier plant to establish their data networks. As we move into the broadband era, it is essential that these two merged industries cooperate in providing service to the user community."[22]

Many of the obstacles that stand in the way of advanced networking will require software solutions. For example, it has been estimated that the scale of software supporting the next generation of switching systems in the evolution of ISDN will be 10 times greater than that supporting the current generation.[23] Given the magnitude of the need for reliable, high-quality software to accomplish complex networking tasks, collaborative development of software by representatives of the computer and communications industries, it has been suggested, may be the most efficient way to address the need.[24]

No matter what the label assigned to a networking issue—communications or computing—the ultimate aim is to meet the needs of the same large set of users. The overriding goal of standards makers and of software developers who build on those standards, Druffel reminded, should be simplicity and ease of use—"to simplify rather than to increase the complication."

APPENDIX: STANDARDS MAKING AT A GLANCE

> The most wonderful thing about standards
> is that there are so many from which to choose.
>
> —Original author unknown

Worldwide, more than 7,000 professionals working in some 250 subcommittees of standards-setting bodies are involved in promulgating, testing, and formalizing standards for information technology.[25] These numbers attest to both the enormous size of the task and to the welter of detail that must be addressed in enabling electronic access to information. Within this domain of national and international standards making, much of the activity focuses on protocols for communicating within and across networks.

The following discussion provides an overview of the organizations involved in setting standards for information networking.[26] Because the complexity and the scale of the effort are often not appreciated, it might be instructive at the outset to give some indication of the extensive body of information- and communication-related standards that already exists. At its last quadrennial meeting in 1988, the International Telecommunications Union (ITU), one of three major international bodies that accredit standards for telecommunications and information technology, affirmed or adopted nearly 1,600 standards that were documented in nearly 20,000 pages of text.[27] The ITU is an organization of the United Nations.

The standards-making arena is actually a composite of many different playing fields. Individual firms—typically, hardware and software manufacturers and communications carriers and other major service providers—represent the smallest domain of activity, followed by trade associations, user groups, and other groups that may form to back a single standard, developed collectively or selected, perhaps, from several offered by member organizations. In the formal, or de jure, standardization process, these organizations propose standards that are submitted for national accreditation. Such proposals are usually assigned to subcommittees of the private, nonprofit American National Standards Institute (ANSI), the principal promulgator of U.S. standards. ANSI may form a special subcommittee to develop a standard for formal approval, or it may assign the task to a so-called secretariat. ANSI secretariats, usually professional or trade associations with expertise in the area (e.g., the Institute of Electrical and Electronics Engineers, the Electronic Industries Association), may provide administrative support to subcommittees. For example, a number of communications-related standards, including several concerning ISDN, have been developed by the T1 committee sponsored by the Exchange Carrier Standards Association.

At the international level, ANSI serves as the U.S. arm of the International Organization for Standardization (ISO) and the International Electrotechnical Commission (IEC), which accredit international standards for information technology and its applications. For example, the OSI reference model and many of its supporting standards, such as those for transferring files over a network or for computer-integrated manufacturing, were developed under the auspices of the ISO. Along with those submitted by other nations, ANSI-accredited standards are reviewed by the ISO/IEC Joint Technical Committee, which develops standards for formal approval by its parent bodies.

International telecommunications standards, such as those pertaining to electronic mail and directory services, as well as more traditional standards like radio-spectrum allocation, are the product of a separate process, dictated by the international treaty that formed the International Telecommunications Union (ITU). Technical specifications supporting the implementation of the ISDN standards are being developed by ITU's Consultative Committee for International Telephony and Telegraphy (CCITT). U.S. telecommunications standards are introduced to ITU for international approval by the State Department, which serves as the representative of U.S. industry and is advised by ANSI.

The federal government also wields considerable influence in the promulgation and adoption of standards. One source of this influence is the government's huge purchasing power. For example, the federal government has stipulated that it will only purchase information technology products that adhere to standards supporting the OSI architecture, specifically those defined by the Government Open Systems Interconnection Profile (GOSIP), published as Federal Information Processing Standard 146.

Another source of influence is the National Institute of Standards and Technology (or NIST, part of the Department of Commerce). Its Computer Systems Laboratory (CSL) participates in over 85 national and international voluntary standards activities (e.g., the North American ISDN Users' Forum, the U.S. National Committee for CCITT, and the IEEE Standards Board and committees). A recent independent review of the CSL's activities observed the following:

> For many long years, the CSL and its predecessor, the Institute for Computer Sciences and Technology (ICST), have waged a long and lonely, but effective, battle on behalf of federal government agencies whenever agency interests were opposed to private market segmentation interests of a variety of vendors in the computer and communication industry.
>
> Suddenly, CSL finds itself in a world where both users and *vendors* are discovering that good standards are in their interest, at least for those areas where innovation is not too lively. This shift represents a *major* environmental change for CSL, and it requires a rethinking of the successful approaches of the past decade or so.[28]

However, in light of these profound environmental changes that open-systems standards portend, the review panel concluded that the CSL's budget is "much too small to address effectively even a small fraction of the topics relevant to CSL's mission."[29] Despite the realities of this budget situation, NIST is extensively involved in promoting information technology standards.

Straddling the formal standardization process are de facto and ad hoc initiatives that seek to establish a particular product or implementation as a standard on the basis of its strong position in the market. The IBM PC computer, Microsoft's MS-DOS operating system, and Adobe's Postscript page-description language for laser printers are examples of products that have become de facto standards.

Users are increasingly trying to leverage their purchasing power to hasten the adoption of standards without waiting for cumbersome formal standardization processes to reach agreement on particular specifications or for the market to cull the array of competing alternatives. Examples include the federal government, as in the case of its GOSIP OSI standards, and the group of manufacturers that organized the Information Technology Requirements Council. This latter organization, together with its highly visible Manufacturing Automation Protocol/Technical and Office Protocols (MAP/TOP) Users Group, has recently merged with the Corporation for Open Systems (COS), a trade association whose goal is to bring users and vendors together to promote the utilization of open-systems technology. The British-based X/Open Company Ltd. is another organization that combines vendors and users to advance standardization and interoperability, using, like COS, product testing and certification.[30] In January of 1991, the User Alliance for Open Systems (which includes representation from over 30 major system users, including such well-known organizations as Eastman Kodak, DuPont, General Electric, and NASA) also joined COS to leverage their mutual interests in the implementation of common requirements for open systems.[31] Overall, there are at least 20 user alliances devoted to accelerating the standards-setting process.

Growing appreciation of the importance of standards and the increasing number of initiatives it has generated are welcome developments, expected to free users from the pitfalls of proprietary solutions to their information technology and communications needs. But the proliferation of standards-making activities by ad hoc groups that have grown impatient with formal mechanisms introduces a new wrinkle, according to Michael Taylor of the Digital Equipment Corp. "A complication, of course, is that it is no longer absolutely clear what standards body is responsible for what," he said. "So, in some sense, we have both an opportunity to do things faster and a new problem, which is mediating among this more complex and disparate group of standards bodies."

NOTES

1. The major consequences of even "minor" software errors in such systems were dramatically illustrated in the July 1991 outages of telephone networks in several large metropolitan areas, including Washington, D.C., and Los Angeles (Andrews, Edmund L. 1991. "String of Phone Failures Perplexes Companies and U.S. Investigators," *New York Times*, July 3, p. A1). See also, National Research Council. 1989. *Growing Vulnerability of the Nation's Public Switched Networks*, National Academy Press, Washington, D.C.

2. Hargrave, Andrew. 1987. "Communications: Towards the 21st Century," supplement to *Scientific American*, October, p. T14.

3. Committee on Physical, Mathematical, and Engineering Sciences, Federal Coordinating Council for Science, Engineering, and Technology, Office of Science and

Technology Policy. 1991. *Grand Challenges: High Performance Computing and Communications*, Supplement to the President's Fiscal Year 1992 Budget, p. 54.

4. Kleinrock, Leonard. 1991. "ISDN—The Path to Broadband Networks," *Proceedings of the IEEE*, Vol. 79, No. 2, February.

5. Ferguson, Charles H. 1989. "HDTV, Digital Communications, and Competitiveness: Implications for U.S. High Technology Policy," VLSI Memo No. 89-506, Massachusetts Institute of Technology, Cambridge, Mass., February.

6. Wright, Karen. 1990. "The Road to the Global Village," *Scientific American*, March, pp. 83-94.

7. Herbst, Kris. 1989. "Getting Graphic," *Network World*, July 31, pp. 30, 32, and 45.

8. Feder, Barnaby J. 1991. "Optical Fiber (Almost) at Home," *New York Times*, March 24, p. F-6.

9. Slutsker, Gary. 1981. "Divestiture Revisited," *Forbes*, March 18, p. 124. Coy, Peter, and Mark Lewyn. 1991. "The Baby Bells Learn a Nasty New Word: Competition," *Business Week*, March 25, p. 100.

10. For example, Time-Warner Inc. has announced that it will run optical fiber to between 5,000 and 10,000 homes in a section of New York City. Initially, the company will offer customers 150 channels and two-way communication features, but the system could be expanded to 600 channels. With additional hardware, the fiber-optic system could also provide telephone service. (Kneale, Dennis. 1991. "Time Warner Plans Cable-TV System with 150 Channels," *Wall Street Journal*, March 8, p. B-10.)

11. Much of the discussion in this section is based on Kleinrock, Leonard. 1991. "ISDN—The Path to Broadband Networks," *Proceedings of the IEEE*, Vol. 79, No. 2, February, pp. 112-117.

12. U.S. Department of Commerce, National Telecommunications and Information Administration. 1991. *The NTIA Infrastructure Report: Telecommunications in the Age of Information*, NTIA Special Publication 91-26, U.S. Government Printing Office, Washington, D.C., October.

13. Keller, John J. 1991. "Standards Set for Data-Voice Phone Service," *Wall Street Journal*, February 26, p. B-7.

14. U.S. Department of Commerce, National Telecommunications and Information Administration, 1991, *The NTIA Infrastructure Report: Telecommunications in the Age of Information.*

15. Kleinrock, 1991, "ISDN—The Path to Broadband Networks."

16. Kahn, Robert E. 1987. "Networks for Advanced Computing," *Scientific American*, October, pp. 141-142.

17. Gantz, John. 1989. "Standards: What They Are. What They Aren't," *Networking Management*, May, p. 33.

18. Kleinrock, 1991, "ISDN—The Path to Broadband Networks," p. 116; and Optoelectronics Technology Research Corporation. (no date). *Key Technology for the 21st Century*, Tokyo, p. 1.

19. *Northern Business Information.* 1990. "U.S. Cellular Markets," December, p. 55.

20. Gantz, 1989, "Standards: What They Are. What They Aren't," p. 32.

21. Computer Science and Telecommunications Board, National Research Coun-

cil. 1991. *Intellectual Property Issues in Software*, National Academy Press, Washington, D.C.

22. Kleinrock, 1991, "ISDN—The Path to Broadband Networks," p. 115.

23. Kobayashi, T., former president and chief executive officer of the NEC Corp., as quoted at World Telecommunications Forum, Singapore, May 1985. (Cited in Hargrave, 1987, "Communications: Towards the 21st Century," p. T14.)

24. Ibid.

25. Gantz, 1989, "Standards: What They Are. What They Aren't," p. 27.

26. For a detailed discussion of relevant standards-related issues, readers may wish to consult *Crossroads of Information Technology Standards*, National Research Council (National Academy Press, Washington, D.C., 1990).

27. Dorros, Irwin. 1990. "Can Standards Help Industry in the United States to Remain Competitive in the Market Place?" P. 35 in *Crossroads of Information Technology Standards*, National Research Council. Gantz, 1989, "Standards: What They Are. What They Aren't," p. 28.

28. National Research Council. 1991. *An Assessment of the National Institute of Standards and Technology Programs: Fiscal Year 1990*, National Academy Press, Washington, D.C., pp. 303-304.

29. National Research Council, 1991, *An Assessment of the National Institute of Standards and Technology Programs: Fiscal Year 1990*, p. 304.

30. Verity, John W., et al. 1991. "Computer Confusion: A Jumble of Competing, Conflicting Standards Is Chilling the Market," *Business Week*, June 10, pp. 72-77.

31. User Alliance for Open Systems. 1991. *Overcoming Barriers to Open Systems Information Technology*, Corporation for Open Systems, McLean, Va., January 27.

4

The Next Tier:
Building Systems of Systems

BROADENING PERSPECTIVE

In discussions of systems integration, even the most intent listeners can develop a kind of information-age vertigo. One must adjust not only to the dizzying pace of technological advance, but also to the political, social, regulatory, economic, interindustry, and international issues that swirl around emerging applications of information networking technology. Disorientation is almost inevitable when, for example, one tries to determine the roles of communication carriers and service providers, an amalgam of local telephone monopolies and emerging competitors, long-distance carriers, equipment makers, and suppliers of information services that operates in a complex, multi-jurisdictional regulatory environment. In short, the technological complexity inherent in systems integration is subsumed by other types of complexity that arise as the scope of networking grows from small—a single firm—to intermediate—a group of firms—to large—an entire nation and beyond.

Perhaps the most salient question at this stage in the evolution of distributed networked computing is, Where do we want to go from here? Building on the previous one, this chapter addresses the question by describing the necessary attributes of information networks as they evolve into "systems of systems" and, as has been predicted, as virtually all types of business and organizational activity go "on line." It also outlines some of the issues arising from the convergence of industries wrought by the digitalization of information.

SYSTEMS AS COMPONENTS

"What people thought of as a system just a few years ago is a small component in what people are thinking of as systems today," said Michael Taylor, central systems engineering manager at the Digital Equipment Corp. "We all recognize that one person's system is another person's component."

This evolution in the concept and actual embodiment of information systems implies an ever expanding sphere of users and applications. It also implies that no information system will ever be a finished product. Whether hardware, software applications, sources of information, or services, new components can always be added. Consequently, there may never be a definable end point in the evolution. And if there is, it is not discernible from today's vantage point.

For comparison, consider the continuing development of the nation's telephone system. In 1876, Alexander Graham Bell devised the method by which human speech and other sounds can be converted directly into electrical current and back again. In the succeeding 125 years, the United States, pursuing the social goal of "universal access," built the world's best telephone network, an accomplishment made possible by waves of innovation set in motion by Bell's invention. However, the telephone network is hardly complete. Today it is looked upon as a component of emerging nationwide and global information systems composed of subsystems as vast as the U.S. telephone network and as small as an individual computer, telephone, or other personal computing or communication device.

"Network-based systems integration is only emerging," said Mark Teflian, vice president and chief information officer at Covia, the nation's second-largest travel reservation system. Truly integrated networks not only shuttle data from one location to another, he said, but also enable assimilation of information, or learning.

According to Teflian and other colloquium participants, most of today's networked systems do not achieve the levels of integration necessary to help the user transform data into information and information into knowledge. In a sense, organizations that have effectively linked information technologies and people have scaled a plateau that becomes a staging area for an ascent to a higher mountain. These organizations, said Robert Martin, Bellcore vice president for software technology and systems, have managed to create network-based systems and, collectively, they face the formidable task of integrating those systems. In Martin's view, at the peak of the mountain they and others must climb is a "national information networking infrastructure."

The challenge for today, Martin, Teflian, and others said, is to build a foundation that supports successively higher levels of integration within and among information systems and, in so doing, increases the accessibility, utility, and organizational or personal value of information. Participants identified some of the transcending features that all emerging systems should possess in order to achieve systems integration on a national scale.

Integratable Components

The fundamental building blocks of an integrated system of systems, said Martin, are communications and computing devices and software components that "can be plugged together" to meet a customer's needs today and still accommodate the incorporation of new technology. A major issue, he said, is the "design of integratable components for yet-to-be-defined projects."

"I think the challenge for the future," Martin explained, "is to spread [today's] networks across the country so that we can do an inter-enterprise automation and fundamentally change the nature of the system to where we build systems on the fly based on components that already exist across a distributed network."

Connectivity and interoperability would not eliminate the need for customized system integration services. The need for specialized applications to solve complex problems and to address unique organizational needs would remain, even with a "highly networked distributed base," Martin said.

Simplicity, Transparency, and Functionality

"Heterogeneity is going to be the byword of systems integration for the foreseeable future," Alfred Aho said. According to the Bellcore assistant vice president, the biggest sources of this heterogeneity are not the peculiarities of different types of hardware and software, but rather the people who use, build, and maintain systems of information technology. More important than the physical connectivity of components and networks, Aho said, are the connections and processes that integrate people so that they can easily use and manipulate information and network-based services. The underlying hardware, software, and networks that constitute a system should be "transparent" to people, he maintained. An element crucial to achieving simplicity and transparency, he added, is a "single-system look and feel," a consistent user interface that would eliminate the frustration that people experience today as they move from application to application.

"I would also advocate," Aho continued, "that we want to be able to develop functionality with which the end user can construct new services and be able to solve problems with the systems. We would like this functionality to be delivered in such a way that a person who is in a particular business can understand it. He [should] not have to be a computer scientist or an electrical engineer to be able to invoke this kind of functionality."

Selectable Speed, Reliability, and Security

Some users of information technology will require the most advanced networking capabilities available, but most will not need noise-free, gigabit transmission rates. Flexible transport of information—whether in the form of data, sound or voice, or graphics—and, therefore, flexible pricing schemes for use of transmission services are so important that Martin and others[1] consider them to be defining attributes of information networking.

Consistent Architecture and Efficient Methods for Distributed Development of Systems

The goal of facilitating collaboration among geographically dispersed groups and among people with different skills and expertise is a major impetus for information networking. Not fully appreciated, however, is the high level of collaboration among dispersed parties required to integrate groups of systems and, ultimately, to create a cooperative environment. The "recursive" nature of the integration process, said Aho, presents special difficulties that undermine efforts to get systems to work together.

These difficulties arise from the fact that parts of the whole—the systems that will eventually be the components of some larger system—are developed by groups that have different perceptions of what the entire assemblage should be like and what it should do. "If you look at some of the major integrated systems we build today," said Larry Druffel, director of the Software Engineering Institute at Carnegie Mellon University, "you see that there are companies distributed across the country, if not across the world. If people [at different sites] do not have the same view of the overall architecture, we can be pretty sure that we are going to see major disasters when they come together."

Eventually incompatibilities can be overcome, Druffel added, and subsystems "can be glued together," but often at the cost of system efficiency.

Druffel and Aho described a consistent underlying architecture as a cornerstone of efforts to achieve higher levels of integration among today's information systems and tomorrow's. Unfortunately, said Aho, "Architecture, I think, is something that we all talk about but understand very little."

Network Intelligence

In addition to collaboration, the perceived benefits of timely capture and effective presentation of information also drive efforts to achieve higher levels of integration. From the perspective of a business, information reduces uncertainty, and the quicker a firm can gather and process information, the quicker it can identify and respond to market opportunities. Teflian of Covia made the point this way: "Information equals money, and timely information equals more money." Therefore, he added, the point of sale should be the point of information capture. To exploit the advantages that rapid capture and analysis of information create, Teflian predicted, an increasing number of businesses in all sectors of the economy will develop information systems that enable on-line transaction processing (OLTP). Eventually, he further predicted, real-time information retrieval and interactive computing will become the dominant mode of computer usage, inside and outside of business. Because of stiffening global competition and the resultant shortening of product life cycles, most firms will view their products and services as "perishable goods," he said, and OLTP systems will be critical to seizing marketing opportunities in narrowing time frames.

The American Express information network provides an example. There is "an absolute real-time requirement," explained Albert B. Crawford, the company's executive vice president for strategic business systems. "As you use your credit card, whether you are in Bangkok or Boston, we have to get that transaction to Phoenix and do some computations to see if you are an authorized credit risk or not or a suitable credit risk and back out to that point of sale in less than 20 seconds, and [transmission over] the network consumes eight to ten seconds of that."

The anticipated transition to OLTP systems creates the need for more intelligent networks, those that are capable of responding to a request without requiring the user to attend to confusing and time-consuming procedural details. Today, for example, there are no complete dictionaries or directories that describe and locate information resources accessible by computer. An intelligent network equipped with a comprehensive set of these aids, according to Teflian, would be able to respond to requests automatically or with only minimal human interaction. Users need not concern themselves with the specifics of where a desired piece of information or an application resides on a network. Nor should differences in computer languages and protocols within a system interfere with communication. In Teflian's view, the network should be able to do all the necessary translations.

Effective Presentation of Information

Making information easily and instantaneously accessible creates the need for tools that manage flows of information and help users digest responses to their requests. While the human senses can take in billions of bits of data per second, the brain processes information at the much slower rate of about 50 bits per second. Therefore, information must be organized in a form and on a scale that permit people to assimilate and manipulate information as they receive it, Teflian said. One simplifying attribute already mentioned is a consistent user interface, which eliminates the problem of adapting to appearances or other sensory cues that are unique to each application.

Artificial intelligence tools that relegate routine tasks to computers, information-filtering and information-prioritizing methods, and so-called "knowbots" that essentially act as information-gathering assistants are in various stages of research and development, and some are already commercially available.[2] The primary aims of these and other efforts, said Druffel, should be to foster human understanding, rather than to overload with information. Moreover, he advised, user interfaces should be designed to accommodate new functionality. Introduction of speech recognition and other capabilities that are in store should not necessitate a major revamping of the interface and existing applications.

AN INDUSTRY OF INDUSTRIES

The convergence of computing and communications and the expanding web of information networks are mirrored by a corresponding convergence of several major industries—principally, computers, communications, publishing, and broadcasting. All are involved in handling information, which in the past existed in distinct forms. But once information is reduced to binary bits, text, graphics, and audio become complementary parts of a multimedia whole, and the boundaries separating once-distinct industries fade.

Equip a personal computer with the hardware for reading a compact disc and providing sound, and it becomes a means of audio and visual entertainment. With two-way communication capabilities, a television encroaches on the domains of the telephone and the computer. Get a "smart phone," and you have a communications device that takes over the tasks of the computer—for example, home banking or conducting other on-line transactions. These present-day examples are only early manifestations of technological forces driving the creation of a large, hybridized information industry. The actions of this industry in formation will steer U.S. society into the information age.[3]

At this stage, it is not entirely clear how this convergence of industries and the anticipated networking of society will proceed. A few colloquium participants suggested that the infrastructural melding of networks and systems is proceeding as fast as it can. Most were dissatisfied with the pace, with some proffering that the more strategic, government-coordinated efforts under way in Europe and Japan will prove more productive than the piecemeal market-driven efforts undertaken in the United States. Whether the comparatively slow response of the United States to infrastructural issues marks a period of watchful waiting or one of indecision is an important question.

SHOULD THE MARKET DECIDE?

Several participants suggested that building a nationwide information infrastructure was too important a matter to be delegated entirely to a large and varied collection of firms responding to market cues and pursuing their own economic self-interest. "If we are strictly market driven, short-term driven, that is a problem," maintained Mischa Schwartz, Charles Batchelor Professor of Electrical Engineering at Columbia University. The tendency to focus on the short-term results in quick responses to immediate market needs, he said, but it diverts attention and resources from building the capabilities and services that may be in demand at the start of the next decade.

Robert W. Lucky, executive director of the Communications Sciences Research Division at AT&T Bell Laboratories, offered a similar perspective. "There is nobody worrying about putting the nation together" on an integrated national network, he said. "I do not understand, for example, why there is no national data network. Why is there no telephone book for computer users?. . . There is nobody responsible for this. There is nobody who cares to do it. There is nobody who is delegated to do it. There is no motivation for anybody to do it, and yet we would all like it." Economic incentives do not exist for services that fall in the category of the public good, Lucky maintained.

But if people are not willing to pay for the kinds of services that Lucky described, the counter argument goes, then perhaps the nation doesn't really need them or other types of services that a national network could provide. "Making general public knowledge available to the masses would be nice," said Teflian, "but who pays for that?" Moreover, sidestepping the market could introduce new problems, he said. "Integrating systems within a company to improve its productivity so that it can compete in the world marketplace is one thing," Teflian explained. "Integrating systems on a national basis, thus affecting intercompany markets, is quite another."

COMMUNICATIONS: A "HALF-REGULATED" INDUSTRY

Perhaps most controversial among the issues surrounding the proper roles of government and the market in the evolution of information networks are those concerning the regulation of communications utilities. Especially contentious are federal, state, and local rules pertaining to the seven Regional Bell Holding Companies and the some 1,300 smaller companies that provide local exchange service. By virtue of their monopoly in local markets, these telephone companies must obtain the approval of state and local utility commissions to raise rates, and the fees they charge for connecting calls to the long-distance network are set by the Federal Communications Commission (FCC). In addition, the federal court rulings that detailed AT&T's divestiture of local telephone service forbade local telephone companies from directly engaging in manufacturing, owning local information services, and providing long-distance service.

The current situation is very fluid and, often, very confusing, given that actions taken at several levels—the courts, the FCC, the U.S. Congress, and state legislatures and utility communications—can alter competitive conditions within markets for communication and information services. Bills and rule changes are pending at all levels.[4] Major changes, in turn, are often subject to appeals.

Within the current regulatory environment and with the proliferation of alternative communications technology, many companies have found that they can save money by bypassing the local telephone network, and they have built their own links to long-distance haulers. Alternative service providers have also emerged within local markets. Some offer fiber-optic connections to long-distance carriers and to other sites within the same city. With a recent FCC ruling, third-party service providers can now connect to the switches of local telephone companies, spawning competition for customers in the same exchange area. The result of this state of affairs, according to Teflian, is a "partially regulated industry." "Half regulation," he said, has created disincentives to private initiatives that would contribute to the building of a national information network.

Using local implementation of integrated services digital network (ISDN) service as an example, Teflian noted that the dispersal of regulatory authority will likely result in decisions that create "discontinuities" among service areas. Large organizations that require nationwide ISDN service, he explained, may be forced to find methods to accommodate these local differences. The challenge, Teflian added, is either to develop a regulatory approach that assures uniformity at the local level or to pursue "higher levels of integration" that bridge local discontinuities.

Martin of Bellcore suggested that these problems stem from uncertainties arising in the aftermath of the breakup of AT&T in 1984. "The United States, I think, is still suffering in post-divestiture confusion," he said, "and I believe something must be done. The best way to characterize that post-divestiture confusion is that, since divestiture was announced, there have been no new national services introduced in the United States, not a one."

Numerous private information services, most serving specialized business and legal markets (through their own or third-party packet-switched networks), have been established, however. Many have not been successful. The largest—and among the newest—of existing services is Prodigy, targeted at household computer owners. Created by a partnership between Sears and IBM with an investment of more than $500 million, Prodigy offers more than 400 data services, including home banking and shopping and information retrieval, and has about 1 million subscribers.[5]

Colloquium participants did not dwell on specific issues arising from the complex and highly fragmented regulatory environment in which the information industry finds itself. Many of these issues pit industry against industry, each trying to preserve or carve out a domain of business activity. Rather, several participants pointed out that such issues prove that government policies directly influence the competitive behavior of firms.

"We do have a telecommunications policy in the United States," Martin said. "It is enacted every day by many agencies distributed within the U.S. government and across the states, and so there is a policy. The only question is what that policy should be."

THE HIGH PERFORMANCE COMPUTING AND COMMUNICATIONS PROGRAM: A STEP TOWARD AN ADVANCED NATIONWIDE INFORMATION NETWORK

Although many colloquium participants suggested that the path of the nation's migration into the information age is still unmarked, virtually all were encouraged by the federal government's newly begun High Performance Computing and Communications (HPCC) program, an initiative jointly conceived by representatives of government, industry, and universities.

"It is a good way to get lots of people excited about the [potential of advanced networking], to test a lot of techniques and technologies, and to show the way as to what needs to get done," explained Irving Wladawsky-Berger, IBM's assistant general manager of development and quality. If the approaches and technologies demonstrated in the HPCC program show promise, he added, the risk of moving on to the next tier of innovation and information technology applications will be reduced. Businesses will have the incentive and some of the know-how to go on to "build the next version and the version after that."

As planned, the program has four major components: (1) research and development work on high-performance scalable parallel computing systems capable of sustaining trillions of operations per second on large problems (accounting for 25% of total funding); (2) developing software technology and algorithms for advanced applications and networking (41%); (3) developing a National Research and Education Network (NREN) with, ultimately, a data transmission rate of several billion bits per second (14%); and (4) investing in basic research and human resources to address long-term national needs for more skilled personnel, enhancement of education and training, and development of materials and curriculum (24%).[6]

Most discussion at the colloquium focused on the NREN, a three-phase project to be jointly funded by the federal government and industry. During the first phase, existing networks linking government, university, and industry researchers would be upgraded and interconnected. The second phase, much of which has already been installed, would develop a 45-million-bits-per-second backbone—the "long-distance" lines of the network—permitting user-to-user transmission rates of 1.5 million bits per second for the 200 to 300 U.S. research institutions expected to be linked by the network. The third phase, involving research followed by deployment beginning later in the decade, would support an aggregate transmission rate of perhaps 3 billion bits per second. The goals of the first two phases are achievable with commercially available technology (indeed, much progress has already been made); the biggest challenges lie in the development of software and supporting standards for managing a large multi-organization network.

The final phase, however, will entail a major technological transition. As a committee of the CSTB has noted,[7] the high-performance, high-traffic network envisioned will require a "clean-sheet approach," an appraisal also used to describe the challenges posed by the less ambitious broadband ISDN, or BISDN. In this high-speed distributed computing environment, even the speed of light becomes a constraint, posing the problem of propagation delays. Technical issues, the committee pointed out, arise in many areas, including network control, layered architectures, communication protocols, switching, routing, multiplexing, and processor interfaces. In addressing these and other issues, colloquium participants pointed out, the NREN project can clear the technical obstacles that stand in the way of building an advanced information infrastructure for the United States.

David Farber, professor in the Department of Computer and Information Sciences at the University of Pennsylvania, elaborated on some of the challenges.

> When you are operating at a gigabit [rate] across country, there are a remarkable amount of bits stuck in the line being transmitted. So the normal approach to protocols that we have developed over the years may or may not work. That is a research question. If they work at a gigabit, will they work at the 2 gigabits that we will probably have in another few years? Will they work at 10 gigabits?
>
> Can we understand what will happen in the future? Big, open question. If you proceed to come up with a protocol that works, . . . then can any operating system we have tolerate data rates of that speed? Will Unix survive when you put a gigabit down its throat, even if you can get in? Most likely not. This litany goes on and on and on, and most everything you look at gets affected by trying to stuff that much data at that speed down the throat of modern technology.

Farber suggested that when computers can exchange data at gigabit speeds, a network takes on the characteristics of a massively parallel, or multiprocessor, computer. The network becomes a "pile of computers that all think they are on a common, multi-processor environment and communicate via shared memory." The optical fiber linking the network functions like a high-speed bus within an individual computer—the set of wires, or bidirectional data highway, that carries signals throughout the machine. Implicit in Farber's model is the need for network intelligence. "There is no way that massively networked computers can operate without a communications system that understands what, in fact, it is communicating across," he said.

"This gigabit technology," he told the colloquium, "is the beginning, I believe, of a take-off point in communications. I think there is a gap now between the 'traditional' slow-speed communications of below 100 megabits, and the future communications of multiple gigabits that people are talking about. I believe the [forthcoming technology] will have a substantial and profound impact on the computer field and offer opportunities that I do not think we are very good at understanding right now."

Farber noted that the NREN's benefits will take time to unfold. "In about three years," he said, "we will understand better what the issues are, exactly what the implications are, and, maybe, whether it is in fact justified as an investment for science. All of us believe it is or we would not be spending our time working toward it and we would not have the funding to do it. While the government is putting in a substantial amount of money, a large part of the burden is shared by industry, which is contributing a phenomenal amount of resources, lines, engineering talent, and research talent. So it is a very interesting vehicle, and it may tell us how we want to do cooperative work in the future in this country."

To the extent that the NREN project and the entire HPCC program succeeds in exposing and developing these opportunities, the United States will have a clearer technical route into the information age. The NREN will serve, in part, as an important test bed for new technologies, applications, and network operation and management policies. Perhaps even more importantly, it is likely to set precedents for many key economic, regulatory, and political issues surrounding the future development of our national communication and information needs.[8] Careful analysis of such "initial conditions," then, is to be encouraged as their influence can extend for many years into the future.

NOTES

1. Dertouzos, Michael L. 1991. "Building the Information Marketplace," *Technology Review*, January, pp. 29-40.

2. The term "knowbots" was originally coined by the Corporation for National Research Initiatives of Reston, Virginia; see Anthes, Gary H. 1991. "Let Your 'Knowbots' Do the Walking," *Computerworld*, May 13, p. 17.

3. Computer Science and Technology Board, National Research Council. 1990. *Keeping the U.S. Computer Industry Competitive: Defining the Agenda*, National Academy Press, Washington, D.C., pp. 26-27.

4. See, for example, Bradsher, Keith. 1991. "Judge Allows Phone Companies to Provide Information Services," *New York Times*, July 26, p. A1.

5. Shapiro, Eben. 1991. "A Service Is Dropped by Prodigy," *New York Times*, May 17, p. C3; and "Can Prodigy Be All Things to 15 Million PC Owners?" *New York Times*, June 2, p. F4. Konsynski, Benn R., and F. Warren McFarlan. 1990. "Information Partnerships—Shared Data, Shared Scale," *Harvard Business Review*, September-October, p. 116.

6. Committee on Physical, Mathematical, and Engineering Sciences, Federal Coordinating Council for Science, Engineering, and Technology, Office of Science and Technology Policy. 1991. *Grand Challenges: High Performance Computing and Communications*, Supplement to the President's Fiscal Year 1992 Budget, p. 8.

7. Computer Science and Technology Board, National Research Council. 1988. *Toward a National Research Network*, National Academy Press, Washington, D.C., pp. 25-35.

8. See, for example, Dertouzos, 1991, "Building the Information Marketplace," pp. 29-40; Gilder, George. 1991. "Into the Telecosm," *Harvard Business Review*, March-April, pp. 150-161; and Weingarten, Fred. 1991. "Five Steps to NREN Enlightenment," *EDUCOM Review*, Spring, pp. 26-30.

5

Prerequisites for Progress

By the end of the 1990s, we will have had five decades of experience with computers. But as with several other major commercial innovations (e.g., automobiles, aviation, telephony, and pharmaceuticals), nearly 50 years of experience do not establish computers as a mature technology; nor do they qualify even the most practiced users as consummate authorities. Many observers believe that the true potential of digital technology in all its embodiments will not be realized until well into the next century. This view was expressed by Alan Perlis, the late Yale University computer scientist, in his remarks at the CSTB's inaugural colloquium on the competitiveness of the U.S. computer industry:

> We must never forget that we are at the beginning of the Computer Age, so that exploration of its role must continue into the foreseeable future. Thus the physical form of the computer may change, but our recognition of and dependence on the abstract concept "computation" will continue to deepen. It is inconceivable that we could function without the computer. Of course we must not worship the machine as an idol but we must domesticate it so that it serves both as a good and a performer. The computer must be expected to play a role in almost every human activity.[1]

Some might substitute information age for Perlis's computer age, but his themes of exploration and continuing mastery of digital technology are no less relevant. In many ways, systems integration marks a new phase of exploration and, as Perlis put it, domestication of the technology. The hybridization of computers and communication technology will yield a new progeny of applications, perhaps revolutionary capabilities that are not discernible from today's limited vantage point.

But these expectations are not shared by all. Some observers extrapolate from today's experiences with computers and related technology, and they are more circumspect in their outlook on the future. The current generation of technology, they say, has yet to be domesticated, and, for now, the need for new types of applications and information services may be greatly overestimated.

Colloquium participants offered their own assessments of the nation's information future, with many generally endorsing measures to build a nationwide information infrastructure. Some described an advanced infrastructure as essential to the nation's economic development. James Fischer of Andersen Consulting suggested, for example, that as the web of computing and communication networks grows, the number and magnitude of the potential benefits also grow. As an enabler of innovation, integration can confer advantages to a single company, he said, "but it also is the basis to give a group of companies some advantage, and then industries, and ultimately, I would assert, the national economy." Other speakers predicted a similar cascading of benefits in education, health care, government operations, entertainment, and numerous other areas of social, organizational, and personal activity.

In Japan and Europe, government and industry appear to find the prospective payoffs more compelling than do their U.S. counterparts, according to Robert Martin of Bellcore and several other speakers. Indeed, Japan's Ministry of International Trade and Industry has estimated that, by the year 2020, the country's planned information network will undergird a full third of its economy.[2] Current activities there and in Europe are creating a political and economic environment that "encourages cross-industry cooperation" on planning and building an infrastructure for the information age, Martin said. Japan and the European Economic Community, he added, are "spending more than twice as much per capita as the United States to upgrade their infrastructures. Each has sponsored cooperative, precompetitive research to define the infrastructure."[3]

While overseas activities may eventually yield returns that could help foreign competitors eclipse the U.S. leadership in systems integration, colloquium participants were most troubled by the nation's complacency about the role of information technology in its future. With the exception of the HPCC program, neither U.S. government nor U.S. industry has contemplated an initiative to harness the evolving technology to bolster the nation's economy, improve the performance of its institutions, and better the lives of its citizens. A study by the National Telecommunications and Information Administration released in October 1991 offers some encouragement, because it both articulates the importance of information infrastructure and considers a range of relevant issues from a public policy perspective.[4] The issues involved are numerous and complex, and many, such as concerns about personal privacy, cannot be resolved solely in the realms of technology and business.

Because it was intended as a forum for discussion of varying perspectives, the colloquium did not strive for consensus or sharply focused recommendations. Nevertheless, it is possible to distill from participants' remarks several major issues and concerns requiring the thoughtful attention of business, universities, and government. Those include the need for making strategic investments, including demonstration projects by the federal government; attending to technical standards; enhancing the role of universities; pursuing enabling technologies; attending to human elements; providing for system security and privacy; and developing a shared vision of the information age. These themes are recapitulated below.

MAKING STRATEGIC INVESTMENTS

The Need for Government Leadership

In 1934, the federal government made universal telephone access a national goal and then built the regulatory framework and provided the incentives that led to the creation of the world's best telecommunications system. Colloquium participants suggested that it is now time to augment that goal in light of technological changes profoundly altering the nature of communication and information. Many also suggested that the federal government can play an instrumental role in leading the United States into the information age.

"What we all want to see the government do," said Mischa Schwartz of Columbia University, "is provide a seed or stimulus to progress in some way. That is what is happening in Japan and in the European countries."

According to Schwartz and others, the short-term, market-driven perspectives of most U.S. businesses will likely translate into a continuation of ad hoc networking initiatives in the private sector, but the sum of these fragmented efforts will not be a cohesive nationwide information infrastructure. Moreover, colloquium participants questioned whether, on their own, U.S. companies will make the long-term commitment necessary to resolve the many technical issues that a nationwide information network poses. An infrastructure will not develop spontaneously, they said, and the decision to build one should be made prospectively, rather than in hindsight.

"Today, . . . I never hear anybody argue about what is best for the United States," said Robert Lucky of AT&T. "It does not enter any equation whatsoever." The nation's telecommunications system, he claimed, is evolving haphazardly, as all activities are dictated by the need to make money. Profit potential has become the "sole source of leadership," he said.

Money, however, is not an incidental item in building a national information network, one that links every home and business. Estimates of the cost of installing optical fiber and associated equipment throughout the United States range from $200 billion to about $1 trillion.[5] Many believe the investment will pay for itself, yielding returns in a variety of ways. For example, one recent study estimated that the ability to communicate, shop, and conduct business electronically over a nationwide fiber-optic network would permit 6 million people to work at home, replace 13 million business trips with teleconferences, eliminate 3 billion shopping trips, and reduce truck and delivery miles by 600 million.[6] The resultant annual savings, realized in the form of reduced fuel consumption, pollution, and commuting time, were estimated to total about $23 billion. While the transportation-communication trade-off has been a subject of discussion, speculation, and disappointment for decades, we appear to be at the threshold of some real shifts in behavior as a result of changes in technology, the economy, and shifting views on important topics like the environment, education, and family.

Because the cost of building an information infrastructure is large and because many of the anticipated benefits might be considered public goods, there have been calls for cost-sharing and risk-sharing between business and government. In addition, the perceived costs and benefits and the magnitude and complexity of the task of building an infrastructure were seen by colloquium participants as impetus for measures to foster cooperation and coordination.

"This is a very long term issue that requires an unusual amount of cooperation across academia, industry, and government," said Martin of Bellcore. In the private sector, he noted, the broadcast, computer, and telecommunications industries "must learn to cooperate if we wish to have an information network." Thus an important role for government is to serve as an intermediary and to create a forum for cross-industry participation.

Martin and other speakers questioned, however, whether a truly coordinated and cooperative effort is possible within today's fragmented regulatory and policy framework. Federal and state policymakers and regulators, he said, "are doing superb jobs within their own domains but, I fear, are looking backwards towards the old edict of universal telephone service . . . . [W]e need to carefully look at how we are stimulating investment in this infrastructure in the United States."[7]

Applications, Demonstrations, and Incentives

The fact that U.S. companies spend several billion dollars on private networks indicates a need for a communications infrastructure. But does this need extend beyond business, especially large firms and organizations such as federal agencies? Still a matter for debate is the extent to which U.S. consumers may wish to partake of the smorgasbord of information-age services that becomes possible when households are linked to a nationwide network. Commercial ventures in videotext and other information services (e.g., CompuServe, Prodigy, GEnie) have served relatively small numbers of customers to date. The development of narrowband ISDN and its anticipated growth into broadband ISDN are largely the product of telecommunications carriers' intentions, rather than burgeoning consumer demand and brimming societal expectations. On the other hand, these services do not go as far as those envisioned for the National Research and Education Network (NREN), which is driven by advanced scientific and technological demands plus concern for the needs of education.

Commitment to and momentum toward an advanced broadband network must be generated by new applications that appeal to a broad number of people. Uncertainty about future markets for information services and applications can impede steps that would further the development of a national network. According to several colloquium participants, national and regional demonstration projects are required to evaluate prospective consumer-oriented uses of an information network. Today, several local experiments—at least 50, based on a 1990 estimate[8]—are evaluating household use of fiber optically delivered information and entertainment services. But whether the results of these trials will provide definitive evidence of the appeal and utility of such services on a national scale is doubtful.

Lucky of AT&T noted that with AT&T's divestiture of the Bell Operating Companies, the United States lost its only mechanism for conducting "pioneering experiments" to try out new services. "We would give communities certain advance services and see how they played out," he explained. "We cannot do this any more. They [trials] do not make money. . . . In the days before divestiture, we had a great mechanism for doing all this. We had this rate-base business where we effectively taxed the telephone-paying public to pay for what we thought would be good for them. We need a mechanism that [permits] . . . the nation to devote some resources to doing pioneering experiments."

The authority and means to implement such a mechanism would seem to rest with federal and state regulators, several speakers suggested. They contended, however, that federal and state regulators are principally interested in controlling the cost of telecommunication services to consumers. Longer-term infrastructural issues and their implications for the general public tend to rank low on the regulatory agenda. Without consumer-oriented trials of advanced information services, said Martin of Bellcore, conjecture will continue to dominate the debate over a nationwide information infrastructure. Whether hooking up households and offices on a network will yield such benefits as individualized education, better health care as a result of providing access to remotely located medical expertise, and new economic opportunities for declining rural communities can only be determined from systematic testing, he said. Similarly, results of service trials could either strengthen or weaken arguments that large businesses would be the primary beneficiaries of an information infrastructure, he added. Evidence, either way, would help guide regulators' and policymakers' decisions on financing infrastructural development.

Existing federal government programs hold varying degrees of value as demonstration vehicles. Particularly promising is the NREN. Beginning efforts to build a multigigabit network, David Farber of the University of Pennsylvania suggested, are in themselves an "enabling technology." Added Samuel Fuller of the Digital Equipment Corp., "Here is an ideal project that can only be done in collaboration with industry, and, I believe, the universities can play an important part. It seems to me [NREN] provides a wonderful, concrete example that will stress a number of key areas that will have to be improved if we are really going to be effective in systems integration. . . . It provides a rich area for us to develop methods, do research, and make progress."

As an additional spur to progress, several colloquium participants suggested, the federal government could sponsor development and demonstration projects that would pioneer applications of advanced information technology to the missions of information-intensive agencies, such as the Social Security Administration (SSA), the Internal Revenue Service (IRS), and the Environmental Protection Agency (EPA). Expanding the demonstration potential of federal systems would build on a large base: the federal government has been the largest consumer of information technology in the world, federal needs for systems have long nourished the systems integration business, and today many agencies have significant needs to modernize their processes and supporting systems. Historically, information technology projects for government agencies such as the National Aeronautics and Space Administration and Department of Defense have broken new applications ground.

Beyond focusing research and development on civilian, or commercial, applications of information technology, federal systems demonstration projects are likely to yield tangible dividends in the form of increased effectiveness and efficiency in government operations, as well as improved decision making. Achieving this promise, however, would be challenging, as such major information-intensive agencies as the SSA and the IRS process information on a scale far exceeding that of single companies undertaking systems integration projects (Tax Systems Modernization at the IRS, for example, is expected to involve technology to handle 100 million individual tax returns plus organizational tax filings, at an investment of $8 billion).[9] For a variety of reasons, information systems at most civilian agencies have not tended to pioneer innovations; they have in recent years lagged the best commercial practice. Nevertheless, initiatives such as GOSIP, for implementing OSI networking standards; FTS-2000, for upgrading voice and data communications (including ISDN implementation); and other federal procurement activities point to the possibilities for a wide range of federal systems to implement and demonstrate aspects of systems integration.

Another option for stimulating investment, suggested by Mark Teflian of Covia, is to provide tax incentives to private organizations that invest in advanced technology needed to modernize the nation's communications infrastructure. To strengthen the "competitiveness of U.S. business here and abroad," Teflian said, the United States must be able "to get past the point of having to deal with the integration problems at the lower level—the physical transport levels of communications networks." Tax incentives might encourage firms to take the next step and move on to higher levels of integration and internetworking, which, he said, would improve business performance and ultimately benefit the economy.

ATTENDING TO STANDARDS

Efforts to develop communication and information technology standards, one commentator has recently written, "are almost always slow, laborious, political, petty, boring, ponderous, thankless, and of the utmost criticality."[10] Such is the nature of standardization, a process that U.S. companies "tend to flay," said Schwartz of Columbia University. "Sometimes we tend to go with it; sometimes we go against it."

In recent years, however, more and more U.S. companies have come to appreciate the strategic importance of standards. Manufacturers and service providers recognize the market-expanding effects of standards, and users of information technology are wary of proprietary approaches that limit their future options for connectivity and interoperability. Unfortunately, this appreciation is compartmentalized according to industrial domains. Communications carriers attend to their own sphere, manufacturers of computer hardware and software attend to theirs, and user organizations that get involved in the process focus on their specific needs. Even within an industry, interests may be specialized and separate. For example, providers of wireless communication services and firms that operate public switched networks have done little to bridge their two operating domains and create a larger hybridized communications network.[11] Thus standards-setting efforts do not fully reflect the convergence and interdependence of technologies and industries wrought by the digitalization of information.

In Europe and Japan, several colloquium participants noted, standards have been made a top priority by both government and industry. The European Economic Community, for example, has created a standards institute to serve as a focal point of standards-making activity. Collaborators there are placing greater emphasis on developing "prenormative" standards that anticipate technological advances and future networking needs, but yet accommodate refinement and adjustment when technology and services are ready for commercial introduction. In so doing, European companies are strengthening their position in the international standards-making arena, participants suggested.

Participants made several recommendations regarding the development of standards that foster the growth of a national communications and information technology infrastructure and that can compete for international acceptance. First, they said, U.S. government and industry must adopt an integrated, strategic approach to standards making. An important ingredient of such an approach is cooperative precompetitive research, perhaps jointly funded by the federal government and industry. Although speakers did not propose a specific mechanism for coordinating standards making activities, most called on the federal government to play a formative role.

"The federal government," maintained Albert Crawford of American Express, "should be far more proactive in influencing international information standards. Government representatives should solicit input not only from equipment vendors but also from systems integration firms and leading-edge users."

"Standards activity clearly needs to be expedited," Martin added, "but finding the right model that assures ongoing open participation by industry and yet accelerates the process is a very complex matter that requires careful study."

Many speakers expressed concern over the complexity of current and emerging standards, which, in the long run, could undermine internetworking efforts and perhaps slow the adoption of new technology. Citing one example, Alfred Aho of Bellcore said the communications protocols designed to support the Open System Interconnection reference model "are getting bigger, fatter, more complex, and more numerous. Eventually this whole system is going to collapse under its own weight." Aho described standards as "essential" to systems integration and networking on national and global scales, but he stressed the need to simplify standards and to increase the speed and efficiency of the standards-setting process.

An important challenge for researchers is the development of so-called lightweight communications protocols, those that entail less processing and, therefore, take less time to carry out their functions than do today's "heavyweight" versions. However, current analytical models and other methodological tools now used to design communications protocols, explained Hisashi Kobayashi of Princeton University, may not be applicable to efforts addressing this challenge. "There are a whole range of protocol issues that cannot be addressed by the existing methodology," he said.

Moreover, internetworking efforts would benefit significantly from wider adoption of programs for certifying the conformance of products with industry-accepted standards and from the development of better mathematical tools to improve the reliability of product testing. However, the former, system certification, is the subject of some controversy within industry centered on how best to demonstrate conformance, while the latter, including verification and validation of software, is the subject of vigorous activity and debate in the technical community.

ENHANCING THE ROLE OF UNIVERSITIES

Given the technical challenges that advanced information networking poses and the systems integration industry's need for a highly skilled interdisciplinary work force, one might expect the nation's universities to be playing key roles as performers of research and as trainers of science and engineering personnel. Unfortunately, this expectation does not mesh with reality. Excluding the involvement of some in the young NREN project and a few other isolated examples, universities have not embraced systems integration as an area of formal inquiry.

Because the field encompasses many disciplines, Kobayashi explained, it "does not really fit in the traditional academic disciplines like computer science or electrical engineering. It is not so easy for faculty members and graduate students to focus on systems integration in the broader sense of the term." That an interdisciplinary approach is required, however, was clear from the remarks of industry representatives such as Jeffrey Heller of Electronic Data Systems, Charles Feld of Frito-Lay, and Fischer.

"Much like the difficulties in making software engineering a legitimate academic topic," added Larry E. Druffel of Carnegie Mellon University, "systems integration faces the issues of definition, codification, and theory." Thus despite the perceived need on behalf of industry, few universities have thus far set up graduate-level programs to address systems-integration issues. Irving Wladawsky-Berger of IBM challenged university researchers and their institutions to begin addressing the field's complex problems or "risk falling far behind the state of the art."

While acknowledging that systems integration is struggling for recognition as a legitimate academic topic, university representatives pointed to some practical impediments.[12] One is the lack of private and public funding for the interdisciplinary research programs that are required to address many of the issues in the field. A related obstacle is the high cost of advanced technology. In the communications area, for example, most universities do not have the resources to make the transition from the old model of point-to-point telecommunications to the rapidly evolving model of networking, said Schwartz. The modernization, he said, "takes a lot of know-how, and it takes a lot of equipment. Nobody is providing that know-how, and nobody is providing that equipment, and so [universities] are falling further and further behind."

Druffel concurred: "Universities seldom have the funds to support complete integration, and most do not have the engineering expertise to build and maintain an operational system."

Heller suggested several prescriptive actions to foster greater university involvement. Consortia with members from government, industry, and academia, he said, offer one means for assembling the "critical mass of resources and talent" needed to address complex systems integration problems. Heller also advised universities to act on their own—"to concentrate on understanding systems integration, providing input to industry, and teaching" the interdisciplinary and technical skills that the field requires. For its part, he added, "business should assist universities in upgrading equipment, share its expertise, and provide input into curriculum development."

PURSUING ENABLING TECHNOLOGIES

Technological innovation yields the raw materials of the information age, while systems integration offers perhaps the best means for making the most productive and widest use of those materials. The competitive advantages reaped by firms such as Frito-Lay and others that have effectively linked information technology, people, business operations, and long-term strategic planning provide compelling evidence for this assertion.

Occasional examples of delays, cost-overruns, and failed integration projects notwithstanding, U.S. firms have pioneered and demonstrated the substantial benefits that can be gained by networking today's computing and communications technology, and they have given a hint of what the future may bring. In growing numbers, foreign firms and governments will seek to capture the competitive economic advantages that systems integration affords. This will mean an expansion of global markets for systems integration services and the underlying base of hardware and software on which information systems are built. In turn, a rapidly growing market will also attract new competitors to the systems integration business.

These developments, already unfolding, could eventually lead to the repetition of a lesson that is all too familiar in the nation's computer and electronics industries. Being first in the development and application of new technology does not guarantee future commercial success. Yet having given birth to information networking, U.S. firms are at least in a position to capitalize on the second generation of networking, during which entire industries and entire economies and societies will go "on line." That these firms will be able to do so, however, is not inevitable. Almost certainly, foreign firms will attempt to leapfrog their U.S. competitors and cash in on growing opportunities to sell devices, software, and services. The governments of Japan and European nations are collaborating with industry on a wide range of information technology research and development projects, ranging from the manufacture of advanced semiconductor memory chips to demonstrations of new information services to devising security countermeasures and privacy safeguards.

Colloquium participants identified several key areas of technology and research where continuing progress is essential if the U.S. systems integration industry is to maintain its world-leading position.

Systems Integration as a Science and Engineering Discipline

"We [must] do for systems integration what computer science and computer engineering have done for computing," asserted Aho. "If we do not do this, then I think the kinds of advantages that we currently enjoy will be eroded, and eroded rapidly."

Behind Aho's assertion lies the widely held perception that systems integration is largely an art or advanced craft, rather than a full-fledged discipline built on fundamental scientific, engineering, and design principles. However, the interdisciplinary nature of the field makes meeting this challenge all the more important and all the more difficult. The transformation from art to science requires contributions from a diverse collection of fields, such as mathematics, ergonomics, and business and management science, as well as software engineering and computer science and engineering. Although many problems can be addressed in distinct research domains, the results of investigations will generally be partial solutions to larger and more encompassing issues. As the field's name makes implicit, integration and coordination of research contributions will be critical to building the scientific underpinnings of systems integration.

What is more, there are intrinsic problems in working on large systems. First among these is the inherent difficulty in designing large systems that will incorporate both automated and non-automated (human, business, or physical) elements. No less a challenge is the innate propensity for large systems to change or evolve over time. For example, 40 to 60 percent of the effort in the development of complex software systems typically goes into maintaining—i.e., changing—such systems.[13]

Computing Hardware and Software Capabilities

As suggested in the earlier discussions of the NREN project, the expected emergence of communications and computer networks that permit users to exchange data at a rate of several billions of bits per second (or greater) spawns an array of technical issues. There is need for both incremental improvements in existing technology and "clean sheet" approaches to networked computing and communications. In hardware, critically important areas include advanced integrated circuits, computer architectures, photonics and photoelectronics, flat panel displays, switching technology, digital signal compression, and many others. Colloquium participants did not dwell on hardware-related issues, but many acknowledged that the future of the U.S. systems integration industry is closely linked to the fortunes of domestic hardware manufacturers. They underscored concerns about the competitiveness of certain segments of the U.S. semiconductor industry and about the so-called commoditization of computers, a trend that favors Japanese firms and other foreign competitors noted for their manufacturing prowess.

Participants devoted more attention to software, which, as Fuller of the Digital Equipment Corp. (DEC) explained, is the primary source of "value-added" in systems integration. In contrast to the uneven fortunes of U.S. hardware manufacturers, the nation's software makers account for over half of world sales of computer programs and related services, having generated revenues of about $63 billion in 1990.[14] This world-leading position appears to bode well for U.S. systems integrators as they venture into foreign markets. But again, Japan and Europe are making determined efforts to close the software gap, focusing on design and programming methods intended to make software development more efficient and less prone to quality defects than are the processes used by U.S. producers. Japanese designers and programmers have been highly successful in creating reliable, high-quality software incorporated into consumer electronics products, and they, as well as European software companies, have proven their ability to write customized programs for business applications.

Fuller and other colloquium participants suggested that improved methods for large software development projects would help both U.S. software firms and systems integrators distance themselves from the competition. Especially needed, according to Fuller, are better computer-aided software engineering (CASE) tools for building "programming environments for system control, revision control, and the integration testing and verification of large systems." By making these methods a research priority, he added, "I think we can continue to differentiate ourselves" in the world market for systems integration.

Two other critical areas, Fuller said, are the enhancement of multimedia human interfaces and development of standardized techniques for managing database systems. Both are essential elements of efforts to make computer-aided collaboration and information networking easier and more productive.

Re-engineering and Building
on the Installed Base of Technology

Collectively, the nation's businesses, government agencies, and other organizations have invested hundreds of billions of dollars in information technology since the 1960s. This large installed base of devices and, in particular, software and databases is alternatively described as boon and bane. With each wave of advance in commercial technology, organizations are finding it increasingly difficult to combine the old with the new, and yet the information and applications embedded in yesterday's investments continue to be strategically important assets. In fact, the value of these assets may actually increase with the new functions and capabilities made possible by state-of-the-art technology, if the two can be made interoperable.

In the same vein, many organizations have a long list of new software applications awaiting development. Progress is slow because each new project generally begins from scratch, even though routines and subroutines that will eventually be incorporated into the final product already reside in existing applications.

Both problems—the one of re-engineering the installed base and the other of building on past software design and programming efforts to create entirely new applications—are widely recognized. Solutions would be especially beneficial to private and public organizations that have invested heavily in information technology, most of which are located in the United States. "By one mechanism or another," Fuller said, "we have to stand on the shoulders of others rather than re-implement from scratch."

ATTENDING TO HUMAN ELEMENTS

While computers are typically viewed as implements of automation, the technology is most effective not as a substitute for workers, but as a complement to the capabilities of humans. However, the computer's potential as a thinking aid, as a tool that fosters creativity and problem solving, and as a means of collaboration is not easily achieved.

Systems integration, said Laszlo Belady, then of the Microelectronics and Computer Technology Corp., "is not purely a technology issue. It is, to a large degree, a human resource issue." But people may be the most unpredictable and, therefore, the most neglected variable in information networking and systems design and implementation.

"I think we are just starting to understand the fact that, really, the computing system has to be driven by the human system," said Michael Taylor of DEC. "So we are starting to think in terms of a new paradigm that says you start with the people, the way those people need to do work."

Several colloquium participants described systems integration as an agent of change. Yet change can be disruptive. The transition to, for example, a leaner organizational structure and a more collaborative work environment may never be realized, as may also be the case for many of the benefits the organization envisioned when it chose to invest in information technology.

Today, however, there are few tools to help ensure that a distributed computing system will enable increased organizational and personal productivity and creativity. Experience provides ample evidence of the importance of training, ease of use, and well-designed user interfaces. But fundamental knowledge of how people think, work, collaborate, and use information technology could lead to significant improvements in the utility and value of the technology.

PROVIDING FOR SECURITY AND PRIVACY

The global spread of computing and communications networks heightens concerns about security and privacy. Once organizations begin to link up with others outside their own private network, as many are now doing, said Fischer of Andersen Consulting, "the possibilities for security violations go up exponentially." If not addressed with effective countermeasures, colloquium participants noted, increasing vulnerability to security breaches could constrain applications of information systems. Yet, they said, the escalating risk has yet to receive concentrated attention from industry and government.

The implications of this situation were addressed in a recent study by a committee of the CSTB:

> We are at risk. Increasingly, America depends on computers. They control power delivery, communications, aviation, and financial services. They are used to store vital information, from medical records to business plans to criminal records. Although we trust them, they are vulnerable—to the effects of poor design and insufficient quality control, to accident, and perhaps most alarmingly, to deliberate attack. The modern thief can steal more with a computer than with a gun. Tomorrow's terrorist may be able to do more damage with a keyboard than with a bomb.[15]

Moreover, the increasing ease with which information on individuals can be assembled, correlated, analyzed, and distributed may undermine the right to privacy, explained Mary Shaw, professor of computer science and software engineering at Carnegie Mellon University. She pointed to two areas of concern. First, Shaw said, information that was once difficult to gather is now easily accessed with computers.

"The second factor that is operating," she added, "is that information that has long been public and probably legitimately so, can now be synthesized," resulting in a composite body of information that is qualitatively different from the raw data from which it was assembled. "This qualitative effect is sort of denied by the people who claim they are only bringing together information that is already public," she continued. But it creates "tension between business interests that correlate this information . . . and individuals' personal right not to have it correlated, publicized, and distributed."

DEVELOPING A SHARED VISION
OF THE INFORMATION AGE

Although in itself an important economic activity and a potentially large source of export earnings, systems integration may derive most of its importance from its facilitating role, that of enabling organizations and individuals to use information technology most productively in applications ranging from manufacturing to government services to education to entertainment. Recognition of this value is implicit in the coordinated actions by European countries, Japan, and other nations to build regional and national communications and computing networks.

While not intended to garner unanimity of opinion, the colloquium did generate a consensus view on the critical need for this nation to plan for its future in the information age. Throughout the discussion, there were calls for vision, leadership, and even imagination on the part of the federal government.

"Leadership is not a bad thing to expect from your government," said Wladawsky-Berger. "That is very different from industrial policy or control or regulation."

If government can help U.S. industry stake a claim at the frontier of technology and demonstrate the potential returns from exploring and developing that claim, this line of reasoning goes, then the pioneering efforts will attract many firms to settle and compete for a livelihood at the edge of the frontier. A rich cycle of commercial innovation can be expected to follow, yielding benefits for the rest of society.

But leadership without a committed following, one that is willing to shoulder part of the risk of exploration, is a hollow exercise. Firms now calling on the U.S. government to lead the nation into the information age must also share that vision and commit to making it a reality. A recurring question at the colloquium was whether many U.S. firms are willing to take a long-term view and to invest in the future, perhaps at the expense of short-term profits.

A firm can be "market driven with the best of them," Wladawsky-Berger explained, "but if you do not pay a lot of attention to innovation and technology as one of the major forces that will drive you to the future, then you really do not have a future. I do not know how you can talk about innovation and technology, where the payoffs may be more than five years away, if you are not convinced that that is very important—that you either push at the leading edge of technology or you go out of business."

NOTES

1. Computer Science and Technology Board, National Research Council. 1990. *Keeping the U.S. Computer Industry Competitive: Defining the Agenda*, National Academy Press, Washington, D.C., p. 66.

2. Gilder, George. 1991. "Into the Telecosm," *Harvard Business Review*, March-April, p. 158.

3. For example, within the European Community the Research and Development in Advanced Communications technologies for Europe (RACE) program represents a collaborative effort to develop the telecommunications infrastructure required to support future computer networks. The program was initiated in 1988 as a five-year effort with eight nations contributing over half a billion dollars to develop an integrated broadband communications system for high-speed operation. (Blackburn, J. F. 1989. *The RACE Program in 1988*, Office of Naval Research Europe Report (ONREUR), Washington, D.C., March; or RACE DG XIII-F (Directorate General XIII). 1990. *Research and Development in Advanced Communications Technologies in Europe. RACE '90*, European Commission, Brussels, March.)

Japan, for its part, has committed more than $130 billion through the MITI New Media Community and the NTT Information Network System project to building a national ISDN network and achieving full digitization of Japanese telephone service before the turn of the century (Bellcore Technical Liaison Office, "Japanese Telecommunications," unpublished paper, p. 2-1, July 1990).

4. U.S. Department of Commerce, National Telecommunications and Information Administration. 1991. *The NTIA Infrastructure Report: Telecommunications in the Age of Information*, NTIA Special Publication 91-26, U.S. Government Printing Office, Washington, D.C., October.

5. Gilder, 1991, "Into the Telecosm," p. 156.

6. Arthur D. Little, Inc., 1991, *Can Telecommunications Help Solve America's Transportation Problems?*, Arthur D. Little, Inc., Cambridge, Mass., May, as reported on in: Passel, Peter. 1991. "The Faxes Are Coming," *New York Times*, April 10, p. D2.

7. The NTIA infrastructure report referenced above (see note 4) argues for increased competition in relevant markets as a stimulus to the development of infrastructure, and it also advances an updated concept of universal service, which it calls Advanced Universal Service Access (Advanced USA). The report recommends:

> Thus, instead of seeking only to provide a specified package of services, the FCC, the states, and the telecommunications industry should seek to make advanced network capabilities and access to non-network based services available to all users on an optional, low-cost basis. Policymakers should generally define, in a technologically-neutral way, the features or functionalities that are elements of Advanced USA. (pp. xxiv-xxv)

8. Lopez, Julie Amparano, and Mary Lu Carnevale. 1990. "Glassed Houses: Fiber Optics Promises Revolution of Sort If the Sharks Don't Bite," *Wall Street Journal*, July 10, pp. A1 and A10. The NTIA infrastructure report referenced in note 4 comments on the lower rate of ISDN implementation in the United States as compared to several other countries (pp. 183-187), and it also references efforts to deploy fiber to the home and fiber to the curb (pp. 100-109) as part of the improvements to transmission systems under way.

9. Although the SSA implemented a comprehensive systems modernization plan during the 1980s that brought its information systems back from the brink of failure, a recent assessment concluded that the "SSA can do a great deal more to exploit the benefits of on-line automation" (National Research Council, 1991, *Elements of Systems Modernization for the Social Security System*, and 1990, *Systems Modernization and the Strategic Plans of the Social Security Administration*, National Academy Press, Washington, D.C.).

The IRS is itself on the threshold of a major Tax Systems Modernization program that will significantly enhance its ability to exploit the benefits of dealing with information in electronic, as opposed to paper, form. That program is under evaluation by the Computer Science and Telecommunications Board.

10. Kleinrock, Leonard. 1991. "ISDN—The Path to Broadband Networks," *Proceedings of the IEEE*, Vol. 79, No. 2, February, p. 112.

11. Dorros, Irwin. 1990. "Calling for Cooperation," *Bellcore Exchange*, November-December, pp. 7-8.

12. The impediments and other issues are similar to those found impeding progress in systems technology generally and notably in the area of software engineering. A discussion of these issues in the context of software engineering can be found in the following report: Computer Science and Technology Board, National Research Council. 1989. *Scaling Up: A Research Agenda for Software Engineering*, National Academy Press, Washington, D.C.

13. Boehm, B. W. 1981. *Software Engineering Economics*, Prentice-Hall, Englewood Cliffs, N.J.

14. Brandt, Richard. 1991. "Can the U.S. Stay Ahead in Software?" *Business Week*, March 11, p. 98.

15. Computer Science and Telecommunications Board, National Research Council. 1991. *Computers at Risk: Safe Computing in the Information Age*, National Academy Press, Washington, D.C., p. 7.

Appendixes

Appendix A
Colloquium Program

January 22, 1991

5:30 p.m.   **Reception**

7:00 p.m.   **Dinner and Keynote Address**

Ivan Selin, Under Secretary for Management,
    U.S. Department of State

January 23, 1991

8:30 a.m.   **Registration**

9:30 a.m.   **Welcome and Colloquium Introduction**

Robert M. White, President, National Academy of
    Engineering
Laszlo Belady (Colloquium Chairman) Vice President,
    Software Technology and Advanced Computing
    Technology Program, Microelectronics and Computer
    Technology Corp.

10:00 a.m.   **APPLICATIONS PANEL**

(chair)   **Jeffrey Heller**, Senior Vice President,
    Technology Services Group, Electronic Data Systems

Charles Feld, Vice President for Management
Information Systems, Frito-Lay, Inc.
James Fischer, Managing Partner for Technology Services,
Andersen Consulting
Max Hopper, Senior Vice President, Information
Systems, American Airlines
Gerald Weis, Senior Vice President, Sears Technology
Services, Inc.

Audience Input

12:00 p.m. **Lunch in Refectory Alcove**

1:00 p.m. **SYSTEM AND DATA COMMUNICATIONS PANEL**

(chair) **Robert Martin**, Vice President, Software Technology and
Systems, Bell Communications Research
Albert Crawford, Executive Vice President,
Strategic Business Systems, American Express
Hisashi Kobayashi, Dean of Engineering and Applied
Science, Princeton University
Michael Taylor, Central Systems Engineering
Manager, Digital Equipment Corporation
Mark Teflian, Vice President and CEO, Technical
Group, Covia

Audience Input

3:00 p.m. **Break**

3:15 p.m. **ENABLING TECHNOLOGIES PANEL**

(chair) **Robert Lucky**, Executive Director,
Communications Sciences Research Division,
AT&T Bell Laboratories
Alfred Aho, Assistant Vice President, Bell Communications
Research
Larry Druffel, Director, Software Engineering
Institute, Carnegie Mellon University
David Farber, Professor, Department of Computer
and Information Sciences, University of
Pennsylvania
Mischa Schwartz, Charles Batchelor Professor of
Electrical Engineering, Columbia University

Audience Input

5:00 p.m.   **Closing Remarks**

Samuel Fuller, Vice President, Research,
   Digital Equipment Corporation
Irving Wladawsky-Berger, Assistant General Manager
   of Development and Quality, IBM Corporation
Laszlo Belady, Vice President, Software Technology
   and Advanced Computing Technology Program,
   Microelectronics and Computer Technology Corp.

5:30 p.m.   **Reception in Members Room**

Appendix B
Colloquium Participants

Alfred V. Aho, Bellcore
Edward B. Altman, IBM Corporation
Laszlo A. Belady, Microelectronics and Computer Technology Corporation
Herbert D. Benington, UNISYS Defense Systems
Kathleen C. Bernard, Cray Research, Inc.
Barry Boehm, Defense Advanced Research Projects Agency
John P. Boright, U.S. Department of State
Jane Bortnick, Congressional Research Service
Charles N. Brownstein, National Science Foundation
Kelly W. Bryant, II, U.S. Department of Labor
Thomas Buckholtz, General Services Administration
James H. Burrows, National Institute of Standards and Technology
Virginia L. Castor, Office of the Secretary of Defense
Al Crawford, American Express
James W. Curlin, Office of Technology Assessment
John G. Dardis, U.S. Department of State
Renato A. DiPentima, Social Security Administration
Larry E. Druffel, Carnegie Mellon University
Robert Elson, House Science, Space and Technology Committee
David Farber, University of Pennsylvania
Gilbert Fayl, Delegation of the Commission of the European Communities
Charles Feld, Frito-Lay, Inc.
Charles Ferguson, Massachusetts Institute of Technology
W. James Fischer, Andersen Consulting
Kenneth Flamm, The Brookings Institution

Samuel H. Fuller, Digital Equipment Corporation
Susan Gerhart, Microelectronics and Computer Technology Corporation
Norman S. Glick, National Security Agency
Gregory E. Gorman, Computer & Communications Industry Assoc.
Stephen Gould, Congressional Research Service
Bruce Guile, National Academy of Engineering
Joseph Heim, National Academy of Engineering
Jeffrey M. Heller, Electronic Data Systems
Merrill M. Hessel, National Institute of Standards and Technology
Max Hopper, American Airlines
Jose Iglesias, IBM Corporation
Luanne James, ADAPSO
Lionel F. Johns, Office of Technology Assessment
Robert E. Kahn, Corporation for National Research Initiatives
Thomas Kitchens, U.S. Department of Energy
Ronald J. Knecht, U.S. Department of Defense
Hisashi Kobayashi, Princeton University
Louisa Koch, Washington, D.C.
Alfred M. Lee, U.S. Department of Commerce
Robert W. Lucky, AT&T Bell Laboratories
Robert L. Martin, Bell Communications Research
Joseph J. Minarik, Joint Economic Committee
James M. Murphy, Jr., Office of the U.S. Trade Representative
David B. Nelson, U.S. Department of Energy
Thierry Noyelle, Columbia University
Don Page, General Services Administration
Raymond L. Pickholtz, George Washington University
Donald E. Pryor, Office of Science and Technology Policy
Theodore J. Ralston, Microelectronics and Computer Technology
    Corporation
Charla Rath, U.S. Department of Commerce
Michael M. Roberts, EDUCOM
Cesare F. Rosati, U.S. Department of State
William Scherlis, Defense Advanced Research Projects Agency
Craig M. Schiffries, Senate Committee on the Judiciary
Mischa Schwartz, Columbia University
Ivan Selin, U.S. Department of State
Mary Shaw, Carnegie Mellon University
Elizabeth Shelton, U.S. Department of State
Fred Sims, General Services Administration
Paul Smith, National Aeronautics and Space Administration
Neil J. Stillman, Department of Health and Human Services
Rona B. Stillman, General Accounting Office

Michael G. Taylor, Digital Equipment Corporation
Steve Taylor, U.S. Department of State
Mark Teflian, Covia
Tony Trenkle, General Services Administration
Philip Webre, Natural Resources and Commerce Division
Gerard R. Weis, Sears Technology Services, Inc.
Robert M. White, National Academy of Engineering
Gerald Whitman, U.S. Department of State
William E. Whyman, Office of the U.S. Trade Representative
Randolph Williams, U.S. Department of Commerce
Irving Wladawsky-Berger, IBM Corporation
Helen Wood, National Oceanic and Atmospheric Administration

Staff
Marjory S. Blumenthal, Staff Director
Damian M. Saccocio, Staff Officer
Mark Bello, CSTB Consultant
Pamela R. Rodgers, CSTB Consultant
Catherine A. Sparks, Project Assistant